Isaiah

INTERPRETATION
BIBLE STUDIES

Isaiah

GARY W. LIGHT

Westminster John Knox Press
LOUISVILLE • LONDON

Scripture quotations from the New Revised Standard Version of the Bible (NRSV), copyright © 1989 by the Division of Christian Education of the National Council of the Churches of Christ in the U.S.A., are used by permission.

The photographs on pages 18, 28, 81, and 87 are © SuperStock, Inc. The photographs on pages 72 and 97 are © PhotoDisc, Inc.

Book design by Drew Stevens
Cover design by Pam Poll
Cover illustration by Robert Stratton

First edition
Published by Westminster John Knox Press
Louisville, Kentucky

This book is printed on acid-free paper that meets the American National Standards Institute Z39.48 standard. ∞

PRINTED IN THE UNITED STATES OF AMERICA

03 04 05 06 07 08 09 00 — 10 9 8 7 6 5 4 3 2

Library of Congress Cataloging-in-Publication Data

A catalog record for this book is available from the Library of Congress.

ISBN 0-664-22764-3

Contents

Series Introduction

The Bible has long been revered for its witness to God's presence and redeeming activity in the world; its message of creation and judgment, love and forgiveness, grace and hope; its memorable characters and stories; its challenges to human life; and its power to shape faith. For generations people have found in the Bible inspiration and instruction, and, for nearly as long, commentators and scholars have assisted students of the Bible. This series, Interpretation Bible Studies (IBS), continues that great heritage of scholarship with a fresh approach to biblical study.

Designed for ease and flexibility of use for either personal or group study, IBS helps readers not only to learn about the history and theology of the Bible, understand the sometimes difficult language of biblical passages, and marvel at the biblical accounts of God's activity in human life, but also to accept the challenge of the Bible's call to discipleship. IBS offers sound guidance for deepening one's knowledge of the Bible and for faithful Christian living in today's world.

IBS was developed out of three primary convictions. First, the Bible is the church's scripture and stands in a unique place of authority in Christian understanding. Second, good scholarship helps readers understand the truths of the Bible and sharpens their perception of God speaking through the Bible. Third, deep knowledge of the Bible bears fruit in one's ethical and spiritual life.

Each IBS volume has ten brief units of key passages from a book of the Bible. By moving through these units, readers capture the sweep of the whole biblical book. Each unit includes study helps, such as maps, photos, definitions of key terms, questions for reflection, and suggestions for resources for further study. In the back of each volume is a Leader's Guide that offers helpful suggestions on how to use IBS.

The Interpretation Bible Studies series grows out of the well-known Interpretation commentaries (John Knox Press), a series that helps preachers and teachers in their preparation. Although each IBS volume bears a deep kinship to its companion Interpretation commentary, IBS can stand alone. The reader need not be familiar with the Interpretation commentary to benefit from IBS. However, those who want to discover even more about the Bible will benefit by consulting Interpretation commentaries too.

Through the kind of encounter with the Bible encouraged by the Interpretation Bible Studies, the church will continue to discover God speaking afresh in the scriptures.

Introduction to Isaiah

The book of Isaiah is both beloved and unknown within the typical Christian congregation. Its passages are read and sung every Christmas and Easter season. People are used to hearing its cadences upon the lips of Jesus as he explains his ministry (Luke 4:16–21). Nevertheless, it is rare to find someone who possesses a coherent view of the message of the book as a whole. The situation in the local congregation is not surprising, given the variety of opinions held by scholars about the book, its development, and its message. Admittedly, it is difficult for the average believer to enter into the debate about the number of "Isaiahs" that are found in the book. Strangely named children and obscure politics do not make the reader's task an easy one. Assyrians and Babylonians all seem the same to us. Sixty-six chapters of prophetic literature are simply too many and too complex, so we despair of ever getting it all straight!

It is the aim of this treatment of the book of Isaiah to provide the reader with an overarching view of the prophetic message through the study of ten selected passages from the book. This Bible study, however, is offered with two assumptions. I assume that the reader will be familiar with the two commentaries on the book of Isaiah that appear in the Interpretation series of biblical commentaries for teaching and preaching. These two works, by Christopher R. Seitz and Paul D. Hanson, provide the basis for this study and offer a wealth of insights for the reader's understanding of the book of Isaiah. I also assume that the reader will have an open Bible. All readers are encouraged to begin each study by reading the passage under discussion in its entirety from the biblical text. Reading *about* the Bible will never be an adequate substitute for reading the Bible itself.

When I was working on my master's degree in English literature, I took a course under Dr. Randall Cunningham at Morehead (Kentucky) State University. The first exam contained a surprise for the whole class. The first section comprised fully one half of the exam, and it consisted of quotes from various poems that we were supposed to identify by author and title! Later we complained about the test, saying that, as graduate students, we were insulted by such questions (even though we did not know the answers to those questions very well). We explained that we had studied hard for the exam. We had come prepared to identify the deep structures of certain poems, to discuss various literary critics' views about the poems, to argue for or against the idea that we could understand the psyche of a poet by the content of the poem, and to identify possible explanations about the origins of different poems from certain experiences found in a poet's biography. We had expected to participate in scholarly debate, we protested, and had been put off by the narrow and arbitrary nature of such objective questions about author and title.

Dr. Cunningham listened to our class voice our objections. He acknowledged that we probably had read much information about the poems and the authors, about literary structures and critical theories. Then he asked a question that I will never forget: "But, if you do not know the poem, what do you know?"

"If you do not know the Bible, what do you know?" The first step in these Bible studies is an encounter with the text. Read the passage of Isaiah first. Then we can enter into a conversation together, with the assistance of Seitz, Hanson, and other commentators, in order to gain a greater understanding of the biblical text.

Both Seitz and Hanson began their commentaries with an acknowledgment that, while a division of the book of Isaiah between chapters 39 and 40 is understandable and even necessary, there is a

---

The Structure of the Book of Isaiah

First Isaiah (1–39)
  Prophecies against Judah and Jerusalem
  Oracles against foreign nations
  Prophecies of universal judgment
  Oracles of woe
  Prophecies of Zion's restoration
  Historical account of Isaiah and Hezekiah
Second Isaiah (40–55)
  The coming salvation of YHWH and Babylon's fall
  Promises of restoration for Zion
Third Isaiah (56–66)
  Prophecies of judgment against the restoration community
  Call to repentance
  Promises of salvation
  Community lament and God's response
  Further prophecies of judgment and promises of final salvation
—Adapted from Paul J. Achtemeier, ed., *HarperCollins Bible Dictionary*, rev. ed. (San Francisco: HarperSanFrancisco, 1996), 464.

comprehensible unity to the book as a whole. That the editors of the series of Interpretation Bible Studies have dedicated a single volume to the canonical book of Isaiah affirms this conviction.

One of the unifying factors in the book of Isaiah is the title "Holy One of Israel," which is used of God in every major division of the book. The holiness of God is certainly a major concept in the ministry of Isaiah of Jerusalem. At his visionary experience in the Temple, he heard the seraph declare: "Holy, holy, holy is the LORD of hosts." In the first thirty-nine chapters of the book of Isaiah, the Lord is called the "Holy One of Israel" in 1:4; 5:19, 24; 10:20; 12:6; 17:7; 29:19; 30:11, 12, 15; 31:1; and 37:23. In the section known as Second Isaiah (40–55), the title is used in 41:14, 16, 20; 43:3, 14; 45:11; 47:4; 48:17; 49:7; 54:5; and 55:5. Of these, Isaiah 49:7 is also part of the collection of poems known as the Servant Songs. The title is again used in the portion of the book called Third Isaiah (56–66) in verses 9 and 14 of Isaiah 60. Throughout the book, there is the consistent message that the Lord is the Holy One of Israel.

The Holy One of Israel has a name that the NRSV translates "the LORD." It is well known that "the LORD" is a translation of the Hebrew term 'adonai ("my Lord"), which is read aloud in the place of the written Hebrew (YHWH) whenever the personal name of God appears in the Hebrew Bible. This term, the Tetragrammaton, is laden with holiness and ceased to be pronounced at a very early time. Although scholars have provided various insights into its meaning and have suggested that it be pronounced "Yahweh," it seems best to reproduce only the consonants of the divine name in these studies. I use YHWH instead of the traditional translation "the Lord" in order to emphasize the personal nature of the God of Israel. Even though God is "the Holy One of Israel," God is not a distant unknown power. The God of Israel is personal. The God of Israel has a name. The Holy One of Israel is YHWH.

It is the personal character of YHWH, the Holy One of Israel, that gives these ten sessions of Bible study their unity. YHWH is known through relationships. The relationship may be with prophet, king, servant, the covenant people, idols, or all flesh. It is always an active relationship expressed through the divine word. These Bible studies are offered with the hope that the reader's understanding of YHWH's personal character, which is revealed through YHWH's relational activity within the particular circumstances of Israel's history, will contribute to the reader's own personal relationship with the living God, YHWH the Holy One of Israel.

While there are several references to various scholars in these studies, the perceptive reader will be aware of my indebtedness to many others. I cannot help but stand on the shoulders of all who have conversed seriously with the book of Isaiah before this particular conversation. I express my indebtedness to them all: those whom I cite, those with whom I may disagree, and those by whom I have been influenced without even being aware of their specific contribution. I want to express my gratitude especially to two of my teachers who influenced me greatly not only in Hebrew studies, but also in Christian ministry: Dr. John Joseph Owens and Dr. Page H. Kelley. I can only hope that I am able to adequately convey to the reader the clearer view that they have enabled me to experience.

Want to Know More?

About leading Bible study groups? See Roberta Hestenes, *Using the Bible in Groups* (Philadelphia: Westminster Press, 1983); Christine Blair, *The Art of Teaching the Bible* (Louisville, Ky.: Geneva Press, 2001).

About the book of Isaiah? See Christopher R. Seitz, *Isaiah 1–39*, and Paul D. Hanson, *Isaiah 40–66*, Interpretation (Louisville, Ky.: Geneva Press, 1993, 1995); Walter Brueggemann, *Isaiah 1–39* and *Isaiah 40–66*, Westminster Bible Companion (Louisville, Ky.: Westminster John Knox Press, 1998); John F. A. Sawyer, *Isaiah*, vols. 1 and 2, Daily Study Bible (Philadelphia: Westminster Press, 1984, 1986); Brevard S. Childs, *Isaiah*, Old Testament Library (Louisville, Ky.: Westminster John Knox Press, 2000).

1

YHWH and the Word, Part One

As a high school student, I was in the instrumental ensemble that played for the school musical *Finian's Rainbow*. Before the curtain opened and the audience saw the play itself, we played the overture, which contained the themes of all the musical pieces that would be sung in the course of the musical. It struck me then that the music the audience would hear first was actually the last piece written. The overture could not be written until the composer had first written all the musical numbers of the show. The first chapter of Isaiah is somewhat like the overture of a musical; it sounds the themes of this great prophetic book. Recording a selection of oracles—which were delivered over the last four decades of the eighth century and originally composed in the reign of Manasseh sometime after 701 B.C.E. to introduce the work of Isaiah of Jerusalem (basically chaps. 1–39)—it now stands as a fitting introduction to the entire book.

If we may compare the first chapter of Isaiah to an overture, then we might compare the first verse to the title page of a book, which, besides the title, lists the author, the place of publication, and the copyright date. This single verse lets the reader know that what follows is a vision that owes its creation to Isaiah, the son of Amoz, and this vision is linked to Judah of the eighth century B.C.E. There is, however, considerable debate as to exactly what is referred to by the superscription: solely Isaiah 1, Isaiah chapters 1–39, or the entire book of Isaiah, chapters 1–66.

As the name of a literary form, "vision" usually refers to a "vision report" that is relatively brief. Most often it will be introduced with verbs of sight: "The Lord God *showed*" (Amos 7:1, 4, 7; 8:1), "What do you *see?*" (Jer. 1:11, 13; Amos 7:8; 8:2), "A vision *appeared*" (Dan.

8:1), "I *saw* in my vision" (Dan. 7:2), or simply "I *saw*" (Isaiah 6:1). At other times, the report can begin with verbs of hearing: "He *cried*" introduced the vision report of Ezekiel 9:1–10. Isaiah's vision in chapter 21 includes: "A stern vision is *told* to me" (v. 2).

Such an understanding of "vision" suggests that Isaiah 1:1 introduces only chapter 1. Further support of this view is the presence of a second superscription at Isaiah 2:1 and a third superscription at Isaiah 13:1. This understanding is strengthened by the observation that other prophetic books called visions in their superscriptions are quite short (Obadiah, Nahum, and Habakkuk, in which the "visionary" superscription applies to only the first two chapters).

> "Indeed, the material seems similar in form and content to other prophetic indictments directed to the wider Israel. . . . One thinks of the woe oracles of Amos (Amos 5–6) or the 'lack of knowledge' theme (Isa. 5:13) in the prophet Hosea (Hos. 4:6; 5:4; 6:3, 6)."—Christopher R. Seitz, *Isaiah 1–39,* Interpretation, 50.

Understood historically, however, the domain of the superscription moves beyond the first chapter to include Isaiah 1–39. The kings of Judah mentioned in the superscription are also named at 6:1; 7:1ff.; 14:28; 36:1ff.; and 37:21. The elements that make up Isaiah 1 are diverse and reflect events in the life of Isaiah up through 701 B.C.E. The first chapter is written from a perspective that looks back over the period of the kings who appear throughout the first thirty-nine chapters. Therefore the superscription of Isaiah 1:1 can be equally applied to all these chapters, not just limited to chapter 1.

What happened in 701 B.C.E.?
Sennacherib, king of the Assyrian Empire, led an attack on the kingdom of Judah following a revolt by Judah's King Hezekiah. The Assyrian forces easily conquered the fortified cities of Judah and held Jerusalem under siege when, according to Isaiah 37:36, "The angel of the LORD set out and struck down one hundred and eighty-five thousand in the camp of the Assyrians." The Assyrians subsequently withdrew and Jerusalem was spared. (This incident will be covered in more detail in unit 5 of this study.)

Nevertheless, the verse literarily serves as the heading of the whole canonical book of Isaiah. The links in the vocabulary and themes of chapters 1 and 66 form a literary envelope or "inclusion" (Sweeney, *Isaiah 1–39,* 69). Furthermore, the concept of "vision" has a future provenance that opens 1–39 to 40–66 and gives a theological unity to the work as a whole. From this perspective, it is not insignificant that one of the oldest biblical terms for a prophet is "seer" and that the "vision" is something that is seen and heard. It is experiencing God's revelation, that is, experiencing through personal involvement an encounter with the active word of the Lord, that brings insight.

YHWH Speaks

Isaiah 1:2–31 is presented as a kind of lawsuit in which God brings God's people to trial. It opens with a word that "YHWH speaks" (1:2). From the convening of court, the word of YHWH is central, and throughout the chapter it is this "word" through which YHWH himself becomes known. The English translation "YHWH speaks" in 1:2 cannot capture the emphatic nature of the Hebrew. The normal word order in Hebrew is the verb followed by the subject. Here the subject "YHWH" is placed before the verb "to speak," emphasizing the fact that what follows is YHWH's word. This lawsuit of YHWH concludes with the announcement of judgment that begins with verse 24, where again there is an emphatic presentation of this as a speech of YHWH. The emphasis there is created by an accumulation of titles for God: the Lord, YHWH of armies, and the Mighty One of Israel. The characterization of this chapter as YHWH's word occurs two other times within the chapter. When the accusations turn from Israelites in general to accusations addressed specifically to Israel's leaders, we are told that this is "the word of YHWH" and "the teaching of our God" (1:10). Then, at the center of the chapter, verses 18–20 are set apart from the rest of the chapter as a unit by the opening and closing phrases of the verses: "says YHWH" and "the mouth of YHWH has spoken." This unit is also part of the lawsuit. It stands between the accusations and the announcement of judgment to make clear the gravity of the situation and give an opportunity to God's people to transform the outcome of the trial.

The lawsuit, then, is made up of a call to order addressed to the witnesses who then hear, in order: YHWH's accusation against Israel as a whole (1:2–9); further accusations that hold Israel's leadership accountable (1:10–17); a central element seeking the genuine engagement of his people in the purposes of the lawsuit (1:18–20); and the conclusion of the trial, which is a judgment speech composed by a final accusation of Jerusalem (1:21–23) and the pronouncement of the sentence (1:24–31). Every element of this lawsuit is marked by an explicit reference to its being the word of YHWH.

> "The divine accusation begins within the widest possible context of calling the heavens and the earth to bear witness to God's charge made against his people, rebellious children, who, in spite of the loving care of a father, are without sense. . . . Israel has less understanding of its Lord than even the most stupid of domesticated animals."
> —Brevard S. Childs, *Isaiah*, Old Testament Library, 17.

The trial opens with an appeal for the attention of the heavens and the earth as witnesses. They are not so much to deliver a verdict as they are to confirm the justness of YHWH's decisions. The appeal to witnesses is common in judgment speeches (see Deut. 32:1 and Micah 6:2). It has been suggested that the background for this summons is to be found in the international treaties of the ancient Near East, such as among the Hittites. In these treaties, the gods or deified natural powers such as the heavens and earth, the sea, springs, rivers, mountains, winds, and so on are called upon as witnesses (Wildberger, *Isaiah 1–12*, 10). In the Old Testament, however, these are not supernatural powers. Rather it is creation itself that is called as a witness. Heaven and earth encompass the totality of creation; every living creature as well as the land and sky can attest to the reality that Israel has broken its covenant (treaty) with YHWH.

> **YHWH Sebaoth**
> This term, translated in the NRSV as LORD of hosts, describes all the forces that operate at God's command throughout creation. The name has also been translated "Lord Almighty."

The accusation makes it clear that Israel, not YHWH, is at fault in this broken relationship. YHWH acted as a loving, responsible parent toward the individual members of Israel's population. It is remarkable that the Old Testament could designate the Israelites as "children" (the Hebrew text literally reads "sons") because the "son" of a deity was a title reserved for the king in the ancient Near East. Even in the Old Testament, "son" of God is a royal title (see Ps. 2:7), although the "sonship" is certainly by adoption. First, then, YHWH exhibits a democratic or egalitarian ideal by holding all of the Israelites responsible for the plight of the nation. Second, the image of YHWH in Israel as parent points neither to procreation as in the fertility cults nor to the common Semitic idea of ownership and authority. Indeed, it declares YHWH's goodness in that God had nurtured the Israelites, who were weak and helpless, to the point that they could stand on their own.

The children, however, have rebelled. The rupture in the personal relationship between YHWH and the Israelites is the result of a deliberate, willful breaking of the covenant by the Israelites. They have refused to trust YHWH. The charge against the Israelites is not that they have made numerous mistakes or that they have failed at this point or the other. This trial is not to convict the people of numerous crimes and misdemeanors. The charge is singular: rebellion. Instead of showing *hesed,* a loyal love that conforms faithfully to the

8

covenant, the Israelites purposefully withheld their faithfulness and were actively engaged in resistance to YHWH's teaching.

Nature, as witness in the lawsuit, must surely be surprised by this unnatural response. The ox and the donkey are not the brightest of creatures and are used to illustrate human foolishness in Hebrew wisdom (Prov. 7:22; 26:3). Nevertheless, the ox and donkey know more than the Homo sapiens of Israel! (1:3). Though beasts, they demonstrate a natural understanding of trust in those who care for them (Brueggemann, *Isaiah 1–39*, 13). Israel does not share this insight. To be faithless is to be a fool (Ps. 14:1). To be rebellious children is to be a capital offense (Deut. 21:18–21).

> "Yahweh will no longer participate in the charade of receiving gifts from people who are not serious. Indeed, Yahweh 'hates' the charade and is exhausted by so much dishonest religion. Note well, what is rejected are Jerusalem's best gestures toward Yahweh. The core action toward Yahweh is prohibited: The relationship is over and finished!"—Walter Brueggemann, *Isaiah 1–39*, Westminster Bible Companion, 17–18.

The People Rebel

The charges keep piling up against the people in verse four. The accumulation of terms for Israel's rebellion is not to delineate the various types of wrongdoing (sinful, iniquity, do evil, deal corruptly, forsaken, and despised). The prophet now speaks to show the completeness and totality of Israel's rebellion. The full vocabulary of sin shows that the people have turned their backs on YHWH "in as many ways as is possible" (Brueggemann, 16). They have gone astray, knowingly left what is right, and engaged in destructive behavior. They have abandoned their only hope and spurned the very one who seeks a personal relationship with Israel based on God's own grace-filled otherness, the Holy One of Israel.

The effects of such activity are evident (vv. 5–8). The Assyrian campaign of 701 B.C.E. has left Judah devastated. The nation is sick. From head to toe, the body does not have a single healthy, sound spot. And things are not going to get any better for this patient because no medical care has been administered. Only Jerusalem is left, and that city's condition is tenuous. The booths and shelters referred to by the prophet are the temporary huts erected in the fields at harvest time, from which workers would guard the fruits during the night. Most often they were made only of mud and branches and offered no real security. What a poor trade! YHWH had provided better shelter: "For he will hide me in his shelter in the day of trouble" (Ps. 27:5; see also Ps. 31:20). Jerusalem knew what it was to be "a besieged city" (see Wildberger, 21).

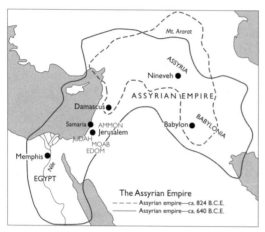

The Assyrian Empire in 701 B.C.E.

Then God wondrously relieved Jerusalem from Sennacherib's army. The retreat of the Assyrian forces was not the result of Jerusalem's war effort or that of Egyptian military aid. It was, instead, the gracious work of "YHWH Sabaoth," YHWH of Armies. There is no triumph expressed in verse nine. There is no joyous celebration of YHWH's defeat of the Assyrian army. In fact, because God is called "YHWH of Armies," there is the hint that the Assyrian troops are God's to command, and this is only a brief respite in YHWH's battle with Israel. It is grace that does not make Jerusalem like Sodom and Gomorrah. The difference rests in YHWH, not in the inhabitants of the city. There is no difference between Jerusalem and Sodom when it comes to rebellion and alienation. Jerusalem stands equally with Gomorrah in deserving God's judgment. But because of God's grace, the trial pauses and the people recognize that they have been spared, barely, from suffering the fate of Sodom and Gomorrah.

Suddenly YHWH's word once more summons attention. This time it is directed to the accused who are identified even more with Sodom and Gomorrah. Beginning with verse 10, Isaiah makes it increasingly clear that while all of God's people stand accused, a special responsibility for the nation's guilt lies upon its leadership. Verses 11–15b address the religious leaders while 15c–17 apply more to the political leaders, especially when read in light of 1:23. The priests in Jerusalem had been highly successful in increasing religious display. They apparently taught the people that the more sacrifices they made, the greater the chance that their desires would be granted. The fatter the animal, the better the reward. Huge crowds "trampled" the temple courts, bringing sacrifices and burnt offerings like gifts to curry favor. The priests conducted festival days, Sabbaths, and new

10

moon services in such a way that YHWH "hates" the worship services in YHWH's very being (*nephesh*, often translated "soul"). It is not sacrifice as such or the cult itself that YHWH rejects. It is rather the empty dishonesty of going through the motions that God detests. Rituals that reflect no genuine personal relationship are, according to Brueggemann, a "charade" (Brueggemann, 17). The religious leadership has misunderstood true worship and has misled the congregation. God hides his eyes and covers his ears to it all. Notice the pronouns YHWH uses: "*your* sacrifices," "*your* new moons," "*your* appointed festivals." God is not even there to share in them.

Civic Duty

The political leadership is just as bad. Those who are responsible for justice and the well-being of the citizens are guilty of violence and evil. Verses 16 and 17 constitute a primer in civil duty for those who should know better. Just like the empty rituals in worship, the failure in civic life to protect the weak and help the oppressed is an indication that there is no genuine relationship with YHWH. But a relationship is still possible. That is what the trial is all about. The accusations of 1:2–9 and 1:10–17 are made not to condemn but to restore, if only the people will "cease to do evil" and "learn to do good."

At this vital moment in the trial an appeal is made (vv. 18–20). The prosecutor addresses not the jury but the defendant! This appeal to the accused is unmistakably the word of YHWH, for we are told that it is so at the beginning and at the end of this short speech: "says YHWH" and "the mouth of YHWH has spoken." At this central point, YHWH is revealed in YHWH's word. What God says is who God is. YHWH is a patient, just, and merciful partner with Israel in the covenant.

The patience of YHWH is demonstrated by the very nature of this speech. Two judgment speeches have accused the covenant people and their leaders of rebellion and failure (vv. 2–9 and 10–

> "If the people accede to God's message in this book with all the resolution at their command, the way is open for them to lead a free and happy life. . . . But if they close their ears to Yahweh's message and continue to rebel against him, in the further confusions of war they will be completely destroyed."—Otto Kaiser, *Isaiah 1–12*, Old Testament Library, 1983, 38.

17). Following such accusations that cannot be refuted, a judgment speech imposing the sentence upon the guilty would be appropriate.

But YHWH is in no rush to pronounce judgment. YHWH is patient and calls upon his full partner in the covenant to reconsider its position. The situation is serious and there can be no further delay, but still the door is open for one final appeal. The invitation is "Come, let us settle this matter once and for all."

At issue in knowing the character of YHWH is the understanding of the character of YHWH's word. Should the next phrases be read: "Though your sins are like scarlet, they shall be like snow; though they are red like crimson, they shall become like wool"? Or, does God say: "If your sins are like scarlet, can they become like snow? If they are red like crimson, can they become like wool?"

It is certainly possible to read the Hebrew as questions even without the interrogative particle. In fact, it makes a great deal of sense. After such a devastating accusation of a religious system whose sacrifices, rituals, and even prayers are called powerless, YHWH challenges the people to try their way and discover for themselves their helplessness. "Your sins are scarlet, just try to change them to the purity of snow; they are red like crimson, make them white as snow if you can!" Whatever Israel tries, it cannot make itself into an innocent lamb again. The Israelites' sin is real; they cannot fix it. God's accusations are accurate; God's judgment is just.

Nevertheless, the grammar of YHWH's word is ambiguous—or better, it is polyvalent. It admits more than one reading. It is possible that God's word is good news. It is not a cheap grace that automatically promises scarlet sin will bleach itself out eventually. God is not saying, "Don't worry about things, it doesn't really matter. I'll make everything all right eventually." There is no cheap grace. But YHWH is merciful, and YHWH's word, which demonstrates the people's powerlessness to change their condition, declares at the same time YHWH's ability to redeem. In mercy, YHWH offers himself as a transforming power to the people, if and only if they choose to change. They must turn from rebellion to obedience, from death to life.

Want to Know More?

About the use of the letters YHWH? See the annotations on Exodus 3:13–15 in Gail R. O'Day and David Petersen, eds., *The Access Bible* (New York: Oxford University Press, 1999), 73–74; also see James D. Newsome, *Exodus*, Interpretation Bible Studies (Louisville, Ky.: Geneva Press, 1998), 15–25; and Terence G. Fretheim, *Exodus*, Interpretation (Louisville, Ky.: John Knox Press, 1991), 62–67. For a thorough discussion, see Rainer Albertz, *A History of Israelite Religion in the Old Testament Period*, vol. 1, Old Testament Library (Louisville, Ky.: Westminster John Knox Press, 1994), 49–51.

About Sodom and Gomorrah? See Paul J. Achtemeier, ed., *HarperCollins Bible Dictionary*, rev. ed., 1046.

About Assyria? See Achtemeier, ed., *HarperCollins Bible Dictionary*, rev. ed., 85–86.

Read silence between verses 20 and 21. The court holds its breath. All that the defendant must do to determine his fate for the good is answer, "I am willing." To be silent is to refuse to live as a full partner in covenant with YHWH, whose mercy proves him just. So reluctantly but firmly, God at last speaks once more. This is the final speech of the trial. Though it is not the outcome for which God had hoped, YHWH speaks with full authoritative majesty: "Therefore says the Sovereign, YHWH of armies (*seba'ot*), the Mighty One of Israel." There is a third and final accusation in which the city stands for the nation (it is all that is left). Every aspect of covenant life has broken down: unfaithfulness, violence, impurity, rebellion, and the complete lack of justice and compassion (vv. 22–23). So this judgment speech continues to include now the passing of a sentence: destruction. The fate of those on trial is sealed with verses 24–25 and 28–31. But even in the midst of wrath, the purpose of YHWH is purification, and by God's grace the destruction of rebels and sinners is not the end of the city. Verses 26–27 hold out hope for restoration and redemption to those who are willing to repent. That, too, is YHWH's word.

? Questions for Reflection

1. Verses 11–15 state that YHWH hates the many elaborate worship services that the priests stage. It is the "empty dishonesty of going through the motions that God detests." Can you think of times when the church today has "gone through the motions" while worshiping God? Why do you think this displeases God?
2. The people needed only to say "I am willing" after verse 20 to be restored to right relationship with God. Why were they silent? Can you think of other instances when God asked the people to change and they remained silent?
3. Compare Isaiah 1 with Micah 6. What is similar between these two passages? What is different? What imagery carries over from one passage to the other?
4. In verses 19 and 20, YHWH was very clear about the consequences of the people's actions: "If you are willing and obedient, you shall eat the good of the land; but if you refuse and rebel, you shall be devoured by the sword." When faced with such clear choices, why did the people choose wrong?

Isaiah 5

YHWH and the People, Part One

One rarely connects weddings with funerals in our culture. In fact, we would regard it as a poor joke should a preacher say, "The things I dislike the most in the ministry are funerals, weddings, and other sad occasions." Nevertheless, newspapers nationwide recently carried the story of a couple in California who had just been married, but began to argue as they drove to their honeymoon destination. Angry, the husband got out of the car and began walking down the road away from his bride. She, in a fit of rage, slid behind the wheel of the car and ran him down, killing him. That is news: becoming an arrested widow 35 minutes after the wedding ceremony! We are therefore shocked by the rapid movement from a wedding to a funeral that occurs in Isaiah 5. We are not alone. It was shocking for Isaiah's first listeners as well.

Isaiah 5:1–7 begins innocently enough. The prophet appears at a public gathering and begins to sing like he's some sort of minstrel. On the surface, the song seems to be about the singer's friend and his vineyard. Anyone, however, who had been listening to Jerusalem's Top 40 in the eighth century B.C.E. knew that it was really a love song. The vineyard metaphor for the bride is found in Song of Songs 8:11–12. Assyrian and Egyptian songs are known to have similar themes of making an orchard or field fruitful. Isaiah sings of preparing the vineyard, and everyone smiles because they know the code. They understand that it is not about a vineyard and owner at all; it is about a bride and groom. They let their guard down because there is a certain comradery that comes from sharing secret meanings. Even today when a group listens to the "golden oldies," those who know that the song "American Pie" commemorates the death of Buddy

Holly can understand "the day the music died" more than those left on the outside by the various cryptic references in the song. Isaiah created for himself an "in group" through his music.

The Song of the Vineyard

The people imagine a wedding as they hear the "best man" sing a song of the groom for his bride. The groom had spared no effort in his courtship to prepare his bride for married life and the establishment of a fine home together. He was like the man who prepared a terraced hillside to be a vineyard. He dug out the area, bringing in topsoil and removing boulders to make it fertile. He provided security by building a watchtower of stone rather than a thatch hut for the guard. He anticipated a productive yield and cut out a wine vat in the solid rock. The amount of effort and the expectation of fulfillment in this relationship were incredible. Then the tune suddenly turns sour. The select vines so lovingly cared for produce putrid, rotten grapes! A spoiled bride makes for a bitter marriage. Whether he was a farmer or a bridegroom, Isaiah's "beloved" already had the sympathy of the audience.

The prophet seeks to take advantage of that sympathy, and as soon as the love song breaks down into an accusation, the singer changes from the "best man" to the bridegroom/farmer himself. He calls to the listeners, "Judge between me and my vineyard. What more was there to do for my vineyard that I have not done in it?" (5:3–4). Perhaps the people were thinking of what to do with that kind of a vineyard. Perhaps some of the more vocal men expressed what they would do with such a wife. The people were involved in the story line and they knew that the bridegroom/farmer was not the one at fault.

> "In sum, the Song of the Vineyard functions in part to introduce the figure of the prophet as speaker on God's behalf. It is Isaiah's first clear public act as God's prophet. . . ."
> —Seitz, *Isaiah 1–39*, Interpretation, 48–49.

Isaiah himself does not pause to consider the various responses of his audience. He delivers the message of what the bridegroom/farmer has already decided to do. The protective hedge will be removed, and the grapes will be eaten by anyone who would want them. The stone wall will be broken down, and the vines will be trampled down by people taking shortcuts across the hillside (a more likely fate for bitter grapes than that of being eaten). No more energy will be wasted in the cultivation of the vineyard, and it will quickly be overgrown with choking briars and weeds. Finally, and with this we know that *Bridegroom* is spelled with a capital *B*, the speaker will "command the clouds that they rain no rain upon it" (5:6). The minstrel is a prophet and YHWH is his "beloved" Bridegroom/Farmer. Who else but God can command drought as punishment?

All identities are made explicit in verse 7: "For the vineyard of the LORD of hosts is the house of Israel, and the people of Judah are his pleasant planting." Isaiah discards the role of minstrel and speaks with the terse forthrightness and imaginative clarity of a prophet. YHWH "expected justice (*mishpat*), but saw bloodshed (*mispach*); righteousness (*ṣedaqah*), but heard a cry (*ṣeʿaqah*)!" The wordplay of the Hebrew has been captured in English by G. H. Box, "For measures He looked—but lo massacres! For right—but lo riot" (Holladay, *Isaiah*, 64). The passage forms, therefore, a prophetic indictment against the whole people of God. In spite of their long history of divine guidance, they had failed to live up to YHWH's expectations. "Yahweh had done all he could for his beloved vineyard . . . but it did not yield grapes worth eating, much less grapes worthy of all this attention (5:2). Nothing more could have been done than was done (5:4)" (Seitz, *Isaiah 1–39*, 49).

> "One of Isaiah's masterworks, the song of the vineyard in 5:1–7, expresses in a powerful way the message he received in his commission: Judgment is coming, is deserved, and is unescapable. It is a highly creative use of familiar images in a way that has tantalized scholars who have tried to find a simple description of the genre. . . . The technique is thus to attract the interest of the listeners by a story that arouses their sympathy or sense of justice, then to show that it is a story about them."—Donald E. Gowan, *Theology of the Prophetic Books* (Louisville, Ky.: Westminster John Knox Press, 1998) 63.

The Woe Oracles

The chapter that began as a playful wedding song now turns into a funeral dirge. Isaiah 5:8–24 begins a series of six "woe oracles" whose concluding seventh "woe" is delayed until Isaiah 10:1–4. The first word of each of these short speeches is translated "Ah" by the NRSV, but that is a relatively weak translation of the Hebrew word *hôy*. A better translation is "Woe!" It is the word that customarily begins a lament for the dead (see Jer. 22:18–19). Just as the wedding song was a hidden indictment of the people of God, this lament is God's judgment upon the whole covenant people rather than a sympathetic expression of grief. Seitz is certainly correct in his observation that chapter 5 is addressed to the "wider Israel" of the Northern and Southern Kingdoms (Seitz, 50). The prophet proclaims that the covenant community is already dead from YHWH's perspective, even though the nations of Israel and Judah may continue to exist at that moment. Their deaths are assured because of their behavior. It is not so much that YHWH will cause the death of the covenant people as it is that the sinful behavior brings its own demise. For this reason, in each woe oracle, the punishment fits the crime.

Isaiah 5:8–10 is a woe oracle that condemns the greedy. The eighth century B.C.E. witnessed a change in the social geography of Israel. Two centuries of monarchy had loosened the solidarity of clan and tribe so that equality in rights and social standing gave way to greater class distinctions. The growth of cities and the emergence of a merchant class with a rich international trade contributed to an unequal distribution of wealth. The old idea of the land as the "inheritance" from YHWH of a family within a certain tribe in perpetuity was abandoned. Amos, Hosea, and Micah join Isaiah in condemning the push for luxury and huge estates on the part of the rich and powerful.

One of the greatest threats to community solidarity was the acquisition of large estates through the confiscation of several small family farms in the countryside. Such efforts were not new in Isaiah's time; everyone knew the story of Ahab, Jezebel, and Naboth's vineyard (1 Kings 21). But crime and violence were not the only tools of accumulation. Hosea 5:10 does seem to indicate that the rulers of Judah used the confusion of

> "The woes are introduced by a term that bespeaks the grief of death, rendered in NRSV as 'Ah.' . . . The mood is not condemnation but sadness. In the woe sayings, there is not even any deathly intervention from God. It is as though the behavior condemned itself and carries the verdict of death."—Walter Brueggemann, *Isaiah 1–39*, Westminster Bible Companion, 51.

the Syro-Ephraimitic War as an opportunity to change boundary markers and gain more land. Nevertheless, small farmers always lived from one crop to the next, so any crop failure, drought, sickness, or personal crisis would present creditors with an opportunity for foreclosure and seizure. This is as true today as it was in Isaiah's time— just witness the demise of the family farm in North America. There are always "legal" ways to steal from those who are most vulnerable in an economic crisis. Greed ignores faith's demand of community and forgets that the land, in reality, belongs to YHWH.

These land barons may well have succeeded in their goal of having it all. Once they took possession of all the land, however, they discovered the peril of having it all to themselves. They were alone.

Being alone in the ancient world was not the quiet blessing of solitude we might imagine. It was more the experience of defenseless isolation. Without neighbors, they could not stand against an invader, and then their "large and beautiful houses" would be empty. Moreover, the scars of battle would devastate the land itself so that production would be impossible. What does it profit for one to amass acres and acres of farmland if it takes ten acres of vineyard to produce six gallons of wine (the equivalent of the Hebrew liquid measure of one bath)? What chance of gain is there if the farmer must sow ten times the amount of grain that will be reaped? The Hebrew dry measure of one homer is made up of 10 ephahs! The very act of accumulation of land guarantees isolation, defenselessness, and failure because it destroys the community that YHWH envisioned for the covenant people.

"Then the lambs shall graze as in their pasture, fatlings and kids shall feed among the ruins."

There may be more to the destruction of community expressed in the phrase "you are left to live alone" than the threat of simple isolation. The Hebrew verb meaning "to live, to dwell" can be understood in connection with the Hebrew verb meaning "to sojourn, to live as an alien without rights," which appears in verse 17. By dispossessing their neighbors of their land, the greedy also robbed them of their ability to meaningfully participate in the decision-making process of the community. The translation of the Hebrew text is difficult and may be unclear, but Isaiah 5:17b can be translated "fatlings, [like] sojourners, will feed among the ruins." The land grabbers have robbed their neighbors of the ability to live as full citizens in their own country. Soon, however, animals will be grazing in places where they do not belong and where they have no rights.

The Dangers of Self-indulgence

Isaiah 5:11–17 is an extended woe oracle that includes "sentences of judgment" (Seitz, 49). Its very length signals its importance. The "woe" announces the death of a community that has ceased to be a community and has become a group of self-gratifying individuals. Brueggemann sees self-absorption and self-indulgence as the underlying concerns of this section (*Isaiah 1–39*, 52), but that does not lessen the prophet's warning against the unrestrained use of alcohol. Wine may gladden the heart of man (Ps. 104:15), but the Bible condemns drunkenness and warns of alcohol's capacity to deceive us of its danger (Prov. 20:1). Clearly, people who are constantly seeking strong drink and entertainment from morning till night cannot be serious about their relationship to YHWH or the doing of YHWH's will. The quest for self-gratification leads them to think only of what they should eat and drink, and they have no desire to be nurtured by the word of God (Deut. 8:3; Matt. 4:4).

Once again, the punishment fits the crime. A selfish, indulgent lifestyle leads to futility. Those whose whole life is the pursuit of food and drink will wind up parched and starving to death (5:13). There will be feasting, but it will be the feast of death as Sheol, the place of the dead, gobbles up the carousers of Jerusalem. When the people are defeated, captured, and forced into exile, only the grave will have enough to eat (5:14–15). The defeats that Israel, and later Judah, would suffer may signal their humiliation and death, but they do not mark a humiliation or defeat for YHWH. Instead, within the covenant relationship between YHWH and the wider Israel, these defeats manifest the very justice of YHWH. God is exalted in this demonstration of righteousness and holiness (5:16). Then, as if it were a footnote, the prophet makes one further observation. There will be at least one other group whose hunger is satisfied although Jerusalem lies in ruins. Lambs, which are alien to busy city life, will find pasture among the ruins of the destroyed city (5:17).

Dragging a Load of Sin

Isaiah 5:18–23 quickly presents a series of four short woe oracles before announcing the punishment that brings about the death. That announcement has a double impact because it is made up of two distinct statements of judgment (vv. 24 and 25). The third "woe" of this chapter (vv. 18–19) is proclaimed over those who trudge along, slowly dragging a load of sin as if pulling a heavily loaded cart, but at the same time impatiently clamor to see God at work! Is this a case of spiritual blindness? The people have bundled up "iniquity" and carry it with them wherever they go. The Hebrew concept of "iniquity," *'awon,* includes "guilt." Some commentators suggest that the people are unaware that as they call for YHWH to hurry up and act like God in their sight, they carry with them a load of guilt that, as Amos 5:18 says, will make "the day of the LORD" a day of darkness and not one of light (Brueggemann, *Isaiah 1–39,* 54). Others interpret the passage along the lines of Jeremiah 17:15, that these words are a cynical, mocking challenge to the preaching of Isaiah. "Oh, yeah? Let YHWH come now and show us the divine plan. Let YHWH punish us right now if you are correct. See? Nothing is going to happen." It's a dead man who talks to YHWH like that.

People who cannot discern good from evil, or worse, who willfully distort the truth in order to mislead others, are leading the way to death (Isa. 5:20). The "devaluation of the currency of language" (Holladay, *Isaiah,* 56) calls darkness "light" and bitter "sweet." It uses speech that disguises actual meaning. The military calls innocent civilians killed by wayward bombs "collateral damage." The business world calls the loss of work for thousands of workers "downsizing." This "woe," as Brueggemann observes, "certifies that manipulation and deception that cover over exploitative brutality will come to a harsh and sorry end" (Brueggemann, *Isaiah 1–39,* 52).

The "woe" of verse 21 condemns those who believe that their own wisdom is sufficient for all their needs. Isaiah was not the first to proclaim that being wise in one's own eyes was the way to death. Proverbs not only warns, "Pride goes before destruction, and a haughty spirit before a fall" (16:18), but also it states, "Do you see persons wise in their own eyes? There is more hope for fools than for them" (26:12). The greatest danger of such self-sufficient wisdom is not that one's knowledge may be wrong or that one's technology might not work. The greatest danger is that a people with self-sufficient wisdom leave no room for a wisdom greater than theirs. Their knowledge recognizes no knowledge higher than theirs. Their world has no place for YHWH. Proverbs, long before Isaiah, instructed the people of God, "Do not be wise in your own eyes; fear the LORD, and turn away from evil" (3:7). Isaiah laments that the people did not heed such wisdom.

The sixth woe, Isaiah 5:22–23, condemns those who value "hush money" over honesty. They are the leaders and judges who should preserve justice, but they pervert it! Not only do they fail miserably in their duties, but they make drunken boasts of being vigilant and valiant defenders of society, regular champions of justice. They are only champions of corruption and carousing! They do not just "call evil good and good evil" (5:20), they also make the guilty innocent and the innocent guilty. No community can survive where justice is turned inside out.

"Therefore . . ."

The two announcements of judgment that follow describe the fate of the covenant people because of their breaching the covenant with YHWH. The first "therefore" (v. 24) employs destructive imagery that is consistent with plant life. After all, the chapter did begin with the planting of a vineyard. This first image, though, is that of a wheat field that has already been harvested. All that is left is the dry stubble that readily burns. Isaiah describes that burning in detail as he envisions the individual blades of the plant twisting and withering just before bursting into flames. Or the destruction can be imagined as a rot attacking the plant at its roots, or as a blight that turns the blossom into dust and thereby robs the plant of any fruitful future. Such is the future of the wider Israel because the people rejected YHWH's instruction (torah) and despised YHWH's word, even though they themselves confessed that YHWH was "the Holy One of Israel" (see 5:19).

The second "therefore" (v. 25) continues the idea of burning, but it is the image of the burning anger of YHWH. That burning anger results in a blow from YHWH's outstretched hand, which is expressed in terms of a devastating earthquake. Could this image have been suggested by the terrible earthquake Israel experienced in the days of Uzziah (see Amos 1:1 and Zech. 14:5)? Although that earth-

> **Earthquake!**
> Earthquakes appear frequently in both the Old and New Testaments. Most of the time, as in Isaiah 5:25, they are illustrations of God's intervention or judgment. (See also Gen. 19:24–29; 1 Sam. 14:15; Matt. 27:51; and Rev. 6:12–17.)

quake must have been terrible to have been mentioned by two other biblical writers, Isaiah is not making a historical reference. His earthquake is almost an apocalyptic shaking of the mountains that leaves the dead in the streets with no one to bury them. One of the common curses of the ancient Near East was that enemies killed in battle should be left unburied. Such curses are well known in Babylonian literature. This judgment may be seen as one of the curses that is invoked by YHWH because of the broken covenant (Deut. 30:16–19).

Verses 26–30 present yet another image of YHWH's judgment, the use of a foreign army to bring about destruction and to impose exile. "[YHWH] raises a signal for a nation afar off; they growl, seize their prey, and carry it off (5:29)" (Seitz, 50). The invader is not named in this passage. The national identity is not the important element of this announcement because the invader is not acting on its own initiative, but is an instrument of YHWH's justice. What is important is that the invader moves quickly, resolutely, and inevitably at YHWH's command. Not one soldier is out of formation, not one shoestring is broken; they are coming ready to fight. Not even their underwear is loose (v. 27)! It may be noted that the lion (v. 29) could possibly function as a symbol of the militaristic state of Assyria, where it was evidently a royal animal. It is more likely, however, that the lion is a symbol of danger and strength that could be applied to any army. It is a symbol that is applied even to YHWH (Hos. 5:14; 13:7–8). Things were indeed dark for God's people because, in response to their sin, YHWH was their true opponent and they did not know it.

> "Yahweh stretches out his hand against his people, beginning with the Northern Kingdom. He raises a signal for a nation afar off: they growl, seize their prey, and carry it off."
> —Seitz, Isaiah 1–39, Interpretation, 50.

"His Hand is Stretched Out Still"

> "We finish with this long announcement of governing themes diminished, bereft, in darkness and distress, hardly daring to hope. That is, in my judgment, exactly where this poetry intends to leave us."—Walter Brueggemann, Isaiah 1–39, Westminster Bible Companion, 57.

Before leaving this chapter, the reader may be helped in understanding the book of Isaiah if two structural devices are analyzed. The first device has already been pointed out. A series of woe oracles addressed to the covenant people begins in chapter 5, but is not completed until 10:1–4. There are seven "woes" in this series, seven being a number of completion. Six, by contrast, is a number that implies incompleteness or imperfection. Therefore, the first readers of the book of Isaiah were left anticipating the seventh and final "woe," but had to read chapters 6–9 before finding what they were expecting. This delay adds dramatic tension to Isaiah's message. The dramatic tension is increased with the observation that another series of sayings begins in chapter 5 and also is not completed until 10:1–4. This is a series of five judgment sayings that end with the refrain: "For all this his anger has not turned away, and his hand is stretched out still" (5:25; 9:8–12, 13–17, 18–21; 10:1–4). Isaiah 10:1–4 marks the end of both the woe oracles and the outstretched hand sayings. Chapter 5 and 10:1–4 set off chapter 6 with its commissioning vision of Isaiah the prophet, chapters 7–8 and their encounter with the unbelieving Ahaz, the sign of Immanuel, and clear announcements that Assyria would be YHWH's instrument of punishment, and chapter 9:1–7 with its words of hope.

Before the oracles of woe and judgment are complete, the book of Isaiah unfolds its plot to the reader. At a very specific time in history, Ahaz failed as the leader of God's people. The focus shifts to a son, Hezekiah, who in chapters 36–39 provides a positive model of faith, but does not completely fulfill Isaiah's prophecy of a Prince of Peace. The fact is that God's people must indeed suffer the judgment proclaimed in 10:1–4. Nevertheless, Isaiah 10:5 initiates a new "woe" not directed to the covenant people. The eighth "woe," which starts a new movement, is focused against Assyria. YHWH never completely abandons the covenant people. There is hope for a new thing, but it will have to wait until chapter 40, which again addresses the issue of YHWH and the people of God.

Want to Know More?

About the "woe oracles"? See Brevard S. Childs, *Isaiah*, Old Testament Library, 46–48; John F. A. Sawyer, *Isaiah*, vol. 1, Daily Study Bible, 58–62.

Questions for Reflection

1. The use of vines or vineyards occurs at several points in the Bible. Can you think of other stories where vineyards play an important role? Use a concordance to find some of these instances, and then discuss why the image of the vineyard was used as it was.

2. Have you ever felt like the ones who, in verses 18–19, "drag sin along as with cart ropes, who say, 'Let him make haste, let him speed his work that we may see it'"? If so, were there certain events in your life that brought about this attitude? What were they? What did you do to change this attitude?

3. Read the parable of the rich fool (Luke 12:13–21) and compare it to Isaiah 5:8–13. What is God's message in these passages? Does this message apply to us today? How so?

4. Verse 21 speaks of those who "are wise in your own eyes, and shrewd in your own sight!" Does our society overvalue this type of self-sufficient wisdom? What are the dangers of this?

3

YHWH and Isaiah

I once had someone ask me about going to church, "Don't you go expecting to be bored?" Author Annie Dillard warns us about taking the matter of worship so lightly. We are wrong to think that we are safe in the sanctuary, protected from the outside by stained glass and made comfortable by the padded pews. She writes, "Does anyone have the foggiest idea what sort of power we so blithely invoke? . . . We should all be wearing crash helmets. Ushers should issue life preservers and signal flares; they should lash us to our pews" (Dillard, 40).

Something did happen to Isaiah in the context of his worship in the temple in Jerusalem. "In the year that King Uzziah died, I saw the Lord sitting on a throne, high and lofty" (6:1). With these words, Isaiah begins a first-person testimonial of an encounter with the living God and the commission that results from that encounter. There is considerable debate as to whether this chapter constitutes Isaiah's initial call as a prophet or functions as a special commission to Isaiah in "mid-career" (see the discussion by Seitz, *Isaiah 1–39*, 53–55). The issue is far from decided. The strongest arguments for interpreting it as a special commission to an already active prophet are its context (it does not appear, after all, until the sixth chapter!) and its closest parallel, 1 Kings 22:19–22, which is certainly a special commission to an already active prophet. There are also strong arguments for the more conventional interpretation of this passage as the original call of Isaiah as a prophet: It is dated "in the year that King Uzziah died," which must certainly be around the beginning of Isaiah's ministry; that Isaiah should call himself "a man of unclean lips" (v. 5) would more logically be uttered before he felt a sense of calling as a prophet at all (Wildberger, *Isaiah 1–12*, 257).

While neither position can be proven conclusively, and the passage retains its compelling power with either reading, it seems best to interpret the passage as the initial call of Isaiah. Its position as chapter 6 rather than at the beginning of the book may well be due to the theological design of the final editor of the book. Oswalt has made a good case for regarding it as a "hinge" chapter with connections to chapters 1–5 and 7–12 (Oswalt, *Isaiah 1–39*, 173–76). This account of the call of a specific prophet provides a fitting conclusion as the solution to the general problem of the sinfulness and pride of Israel that the first five chapters introduce. At the same time, the specific calling is just the beginning of what is a more "autobiographical/biographical" account of the career of the prophet Isaiah and his encounters with Judah's kings, not only in chapters 7–12 but also in the larger unit of chapters 7–39.

Another debated issue is whether or not Isaiah was in the temple when he experienced this vision. Of course one cannot dogmatically claim to have reached the absolute correct decision because there is nothing to preclude the possibility of a prophet having a vision while in the comfort of his own bed, while traveling alone down a dirt road, or while on vacation at the seashore with his family. Nevertheless, it is probable, given the details of the "pivots on the thresholds" and "smoke" and "live coal" from the incense altar, that Isaiah did experience his vision of YHWH and the heavenly throne room within the temple precincts (Wildberger, *Isaiah 1–12*, 263). That is certainly the point of the vision in chapter 6. Unlike the account of Micaiah's vision in 1 Kings 22, the point is not simply to place the prophet in the heavenly court in order to give his message authority. Isaiah's vision is connected with the death of Israel's king, Uzziah, and its content is a personal encounter with the living, eternal King, YHWH Sebaoth (6:5). The Hebrew word *hêkal* may be translated as "temple" or "palace." It is theologically vital that Isaiah's vision occurred at the place where heaven and earth intersect, in YHWH's temple/palace located in Jerusalem. Earthly kings live and die, but YHWH is eternally on the throne. Small kingdoms may be threatened by Assyrian kings and their armies, but YHWH Sebaoth (Lord of hosts or Lord of armies) is King over all kingdoms and is Commander over all armies. The vision offers stability in the time of crisis.

A Vulnerable Kingdom

The death of Uzziah marked a particularly vulnerable moment for Judah. He had been king for more than forty years and had led Judah to enjoy its greatest level of peace and prosperity since the Davidic empire divided after the death of Solomon. Uzziah and Jeroboam II had achieved peace between Judah and Israel and led their countries through a period of national restoration and expansion. Although Uzziah suffered from leprosy the last few years of his life and therefore shared the throne with his son and successor, Jotham, Uzziah remained a popular ruler. His death would have naturally given rise to fears and questions about policy shifts in even the calmest of times, but it occurred around the same time as the resurgence of the Assyrian empire under Tiglath–pileser III in 745 B.C.E. Fears about the future were at an all-time high when Isaiah saw "the Lord sitting on a throne, high and lofty" (Isaiah 6:1).

God, according to Isaiah's vision, certainly is "high and lofty." No one can see YHWH face to face and live (Ex. 33:20), so Isaiah's description of the Almighty goes no higher than the hem of YHWH's robe, which in itself is sufficient to fill the temple. The heavenly King is not without court attendants. At least two seraphs hover near at hand. We really have no full description of these six-winged creatures, although they are often described as serpentlike because of their association with snakes in Isaiah 14:29 and 30:6. They have also been identified with the Ñfr, a fabled Egyptian winged creature, and have been described as composite creatures with human/serpent/bird features (Wildberger, 264). The word "seraph" comes from the Hebrew verb for "burning," so some kind of association with the fire as a symbol of divine presence, holiness, and purification seems assured.

The seraphs are engaged in a song of praise to YHWH that has two key words: "holy" and "glory." YHWH is holy. That the seraphs repeat the word three times signifies the absolute quality of God's holiness. "Holy" does not denote primarily that something exhibits an ethical purity. It is a term that first of all marks something apart from the ordinary or common. It signifies that which is characteristic and special with regard to God. What is holy is separate. The seraphs' song affirms "God's absolute distinctiveness, his distance from any share in the ordinariness of the world" (Holladay, *Isaiah,* 30). There is a total and complete otherness when it comes to God in relation to humanity. At the same time, the song celebrates the fact that God's "glory" fills all the earth. The word "glory" in Hebrew (*kabod*) comes from the verb meaning "to be heavy." God carries weight in the world. "Glory" can signify the visible evidence of God's presence (Ezek. 10:18–19; 43:4–5). The hymn of worship sung by the seraphs

27

affirms a paradox. God, the inmost nature of God, is absolutely other, majestic, inscrutable, and unsearchable. Yet God, the revealed nature

"Woe is me! I am lost, for I am a man of unclean lips."

of God, is preeminently present in the world and all who do not recognize and respond with honor toward the One revealed through creation are without excuse (cf. Romans 1:19–21).

Was it the volume or the significance of the seraphs' singing that caused the very threshold of the temple to shake? Was the smoke that of incense being burned on the altar or was it the dragon breath of the fiery seraphs that filled the temple? At any rate, Isaiah was aware of the presence of God in worship through every sense: He heard the song, he felt the shaking, and he could see, smell, and taste the smoke. This worship of YHWH could be hazardous! The prophet cries out, "Woe is me! I am lost" (6:5). It is a terrifying thing to be thrust into the presence of God.

Is it safe?

C. S. Lewis shed some insight into the worship of the awe-inspiring God in his book *The Lion, the Witch and the Wardrobe.* The children of the story are in the company of Mr. and Mrs. Beaver, who tell them about Aslan. They discover that Aslan is king and that Aslan is a lion. The children are scared because Aslan is not a man, he is a lion, and they wonder if he is safe. "'Safe?' said Mr. Beaver. 'Don't you hear what Mrs. Beaver tells you? Who said anything about safe? 'Course he isn't safe. But he's good. He's the King, I tell you'" (Lewis, 86). Isaiah discovered that there is nothing safe about the Holy One of Israel. The worship of God is no "buddy-buddy" relationship. Unholiness cannot survive the Holy. Not-good cannot endure the Good. "Woe!" is the cry of a funeral dirge. Isaiah counted himself as good as dead.

Isaiah expressed his sense of guilt and unworthiness before the Holy One of Israel by calling himself a person of "unclean lips" (6:5). Of course, "lips" is a poetic device in which the part stands for the whole; Isaiah knows that he is wholly unclean. It is significant, however, that he chose to express his condition by drawing attention to his lips. A prophet is God's spokesperson. As a prophet, Isaiah could be faithful only by speaking those words that God put on his lips. Until this moment, Isaiah says, his lips have borne words that cannot survive in the presence of God. The very cry of Isaiah can be translated, "Woe is me! I am silenced." The Hebrew verb *damah* can carry the meaning of destruction or that of silence (Clines, ed., *Dictionary of Classical Hebrew*, vol. 2, p. 448). Isaiah may be playing with both meanings: He feels crushed by his guilt and therefore has been struck dumb before God (Holladay, *Isaiah*, 31–32). How can he be a prophet if he cannot speak?

> "'Safe?' said Mr. Beaver. 'Don't you hear what Mrs. Beaver tells you? Who said anything about safe? 'Course he isn't safe. But he's good. He's the King, I tell you.'"— C. S. Lewis, *The Lion, the Witch, and the Wardrobe* (New York: Collier Books, 1970).

Isaiah is not alone. He lives "among a people of unclean lips." The words of the covenant people have no place in the presence of YHWH. The people themselves are unclean because of their words. The Hebrew concept of "word," *dabar*, is larger than our own. *Dabar* means "thing," "deed," "event," or "manner," as well as "word" (Clines, *Dictionary of Classical Hebrew*, vol. 2, 397). Once a word is spoken, it takes on an existence of its own as an event with a power to bring itself into fulfillment as an action. Therefore, the "people of unclean lips" are unclean in thought, speech, and activity. Uzziah, though a king, had been a leper. He was "unclean" and had been separated from his people, ruling through his son Jotham, who acted as co-regent. But the whole nation shared in the uncleanness of its king. Before the holy God, everyone, even Isaiah, was unfit and polluted (Holladay, *Isaiah*, 33). Their disability, however, was not the result of the occurrence of a disease like Uzziah suffered. It was the deliberate act of rebellion.

"Whom Shall I Send?"

The holiness of God is not a limitation. God is able to act on behalf of those who have disqualified themselves from service. One of the seraphs takes a live coal from the golden incense altar with a pair of tongs (it must have been too hot even for this fiery creature to handle) and touches the lips of Isaiah with the hot coal. With that grace-filled action of purification, the announcement is made that Isaiah's guilt and sin have been dealt with completely. The forgiveness was God's act; there was nothing that Isaiah did or could have done about it himself. The divine action is decisive because, as Seitz points out, Isaiah is now made distinct from the rest of the unclean nation and "he is free to step forward and respond when God calls" (Seitz, *Isaiah 1–39*, 55). Indeed, Isaiah then overheard a discussion in the heavenly throne room. YHWH was saying, "Whom shall I send, and who will go for us?" And Isaiah volunteered!

> "Then I heard the voice of the LORD saying, 'Whom shall I send, and who will go for us?' And I said, 'Here I am; send me!'"
> —Isaiah 6:8.

Immediately Isaiah's offer is accepted and he is commissioned with a message. Now we do not know too much about Isaiah. We know his father's name and the names of at least two of his children. We know he was married, but we are unaware of his wife's name. There is only a legend about his death, being sawn in two by King Manasseh. We do not know much about this preacher, but we surely do remember his message! The message that Isaiah is given here to proclaim is so jarring that it makes us want to install airbags as well as seatbelts for our worship of God. Isaiah's message to the people is to be the following: "Keep listening, but do not comprehend; keep looking, but do not understand" (6:9). Isaiah's sermons are to "make the mind of this people dull, and stop their ears, and shut their eyes, so that they may not look . . . and listen . . . and comprehend . . . and turn and be healed" (6:10).

Who was Isaiah?

Isaiah was a prophet of Judah during the reigns of kings Uzziah, Jotham, Ahaz, and Hezekiah, dating from roughly 740 to 700 B.C.E. He lived in Jerusalem and was married to a woman he called a "prophetess," with whom he had at least two sons. He was a contemporary of the prophet Micah and was preceded slightly by the prophets Amos and Hosea. There is some speculation that Isaiah was martyred by King Manasseh, and that Hebrews 11:37 ("they were sawn in two") alludes to his death.

Isaiah's response to this commission is: "How long?" The question is not simply one for information: "Do I preach this message for seven months or for seven years?" The question itself is an element common in complaint Psalms (Pss. 13:1–2; 35:17; 74:10; 79:5; 89:46; etc.). It is very much like the slogan adopted by a political party during the Peruvian elections in the mid-1980s. The "United Left" party was a coalition of various leftist groups including the Communist party. Their campaign slogan was the question, *Hasta cuando?*— "How long?" Literally, the English translation is "Until when?" The question did not want a particular date for an answer. It was a social protest that expected change because the people deserved better. It was not something asked as much as a shout of anticipation that the people would mobilize and effect the needed reforms. Isaiah's "Until when?" is also a protest, an expectation that this is not all there is to God's message, an anticipation that this is not all there is to God's holiness.

"Until!"

The answer to Isaiah's "Until?" is YHWH's "Until!" While Isaiah's question anticipated something more, YHWH would allow no short-cuts. Nothing would be allowed to short-circuit God's dealings with the people of the covenant. The answer is: "As long as it takes. Until the task is completed. Until the job is thoroughly done." The task at hand is the judgment of God's people. They are after all a "people of unclean lips" who claim to live in the presence of the Holy One of Israel. It may be true that the purpose of God's judgment is purification, reconciliation, and redemption, but it is inescapably judgment. It cannot be bypassed, and it may seem harsh. In a sermon on the book of Hebrews, Dr. Fred Craddock alluded to the vinedresser of John 15. I remember that Dr. Craddock described the vinedresser going into the vineyard with a big, curved pruning knife. Sometimes he would cut off branches that were unfruitful and without value. At other times, he would prune parts of the vine so that the branch could grow better and be more fruitful. Then Dr. Craddock said something like, "Now, the vine doesn't know if it is being cut off and discarded because it is fruitless, or if it is being cut in an effort to prune it and make it more fruitful. In either case, the knife feels the same." The judgment of God, whatever may be its goal or its result, always feels like the end (6:11–12). Isaiah is told that this time, the judgment will be especially keen: "Even if a tenth part remain in

> "When the prophet has been forgiven, he overhears a dialogue between God and his heavenly court . . . which he is inspired to interrupt and answer by offering himself. He then finds himself, like Moses (Exod. 3:10–11), and indeed Jeremiah (1:4–8), faced with an impossible task as a prophet of the Lord."—John F. A. Sawyer, *Isaiah*, vol. 1, *Daily Study Bible*, 72.

it, it will be burned again, like a terebinth or an oak whose stump remains standing when it is felled" (6:13a–b). Nothing can lighten the awesome burden of God's judgment.

Complete judgment is not all there is to YHWH's "Until!" The Hebrew of verse 6:13c consists of three words meaning, literally, in English, "Seed of holiness its stump." The words are enigmatic; they constitute a puzzlement. Nevertheless, they point toward a hope that the trust expressed in Isaiah's "How long?"—that there was more to God's holiness than destruction—may not have been wrong. Three words do not hold out much hope, but it is hope nonetheless. Isaiah's own experience argues that it is not a false hope. Isaiah himself was "a person of unclean lips" living in the middle of this people of unclean lips. God encountered him with grace, forgiveness, and purification. Could the same thing not be in store for all of Israel? Isaiah experienced the burning of a coal in that process. Must not even the stump left by Assyria also undergo a burning before the process is complete? While YHWH's "Until!" provides no details, it at least offers something.

The Full Judgment of YHWH

Why should YHWH talk like this to Isaiah? Couldn't things be at least a little clearer? Would God really call on a prophet to make minds dull, ears stopped, eyes blind, and hearts unresponsive? (Surely we preachers do that too often on our own, without any help from God!) Some interpreters have dealt with the problem by suggesting that this account of Isaiah's call was given shape only toward the end of Isaiah's ministry. That is, chapter 6 is a reflective account of the call made from the perspective of a mature Isaiah who knew all the heartbreaks, failures, and difficulties that his ministry had involved. Isaiah knew he was genuinely called by God, and he knew the results of his preaching were often rejection and disinterest. Therefore, he concluded and reported that this must have been God's plan from the very beginning. This type of explanation continues to be popular, but it seems to miss the force of Isaiah's complaint, "How long, O Lord?" The very question suggests that Isaiah was aware of this aspect of his ministry from the beginning. Others try to deflect the force of these words by suggest-

> "How could God charge Isaiah to so dull the hearts of his people that they could not turn and be healed?"—Seitz, *Isaiah 1–39,* 55.

ing that they were originally spoken only about the Northern Kingdom, Israel, or that they are to be read as sarcasm (Holladay, *Isaiah*, 37–38).

Seitz has come up with the best clue for an adequate reading of these words. He points out that these words are addressed personally to Isaiah, and he suggests that their purpose is a pastoral one on the part of YHWH toward Isaiah (Seitz, *Isaiah 1–39*, 56). It is as if God draws Isaiah aside before sending him from the heavenly council and into the fight to tell him not to consider the response that he will receive toward his preaching as a failure. Even the rejection and dullness of his listeners have been taken into account by YHWH within the divine scheme of things. YHWH stands with the prophet, YHWH honors the prophetic message, and YHWH will successfully use Isaiah's ministry in Israel's future, even if it largely fails in this present generation.

> "Isaiah is not to interpret the refusal to hear, which comes as a result of his preaching, as a sign of failure or as an indication of divine malfeasance. The prophet learns from God that he will make hearts fat with the effect that the people will not turn and be healed. God lets him know this at a critical moment in his career, as he is about to leave the divine council."—Seitz, *Isaiah 1–39*, Interpretation, 56.

Isaiah is called by YHWH to be instrumental in bringing the encounter between God and God's people to the point of reckoning. Just as those guilty of substance abuse often deny their dependence on alcohol or drugs, the people of Judah lived in denial of a problem in their relationship with YHWH. As long as addicts are protected from the consequences of their own actions by well-meaning loved ones, they have no incentive to improve their condition. Many times, they have to reach rock bottom before the opportunity for real change even exists. In a similar manner, Judah could not be brought into a right relationship with God through a cheap grace and an easy forgiveness. Sin is not meaningless. To have the possibility of living in right relationship with YHWH, Judah had to experience the full judgment of YHWH. Then, and only then, would there be real hope. In the visionary event of his calling, Isaiah experienced what YHWH had in store for the people of Judah and was commissioned to proclaim that message with nothing held back. Harsh. But in its very severity lies Israel's only hope.

 Want to Know More?

About the call of the prophets? See Horst Dietrich Preuss, *Old Testament Theology*, vol. 2 (Louisville, Ky.: Westminster John Knox Press, 1996), 67–69; Brevard S. Childs, *Isaiah*, Old Testament Library, 52–53.

About the reign of King Uzziah? See Paul J. Achtemeier, ed., *HarperCollins Bible Dictionary*, rev. ed., 1188–89.

? Questions for Reflection

1. Scholars debate whether Isaiah was in the temple when he experienced this vision. Do you think the location of the vision in this passage is important? Why or why not?

2. The exchange between YHWH and Isaiah in 6:8 is one of the most memorable passages in the Old Testament. It is also a passage that makes us a bit nervous—what if God asks us, "Whom shall I send?" Have you ever experienced this type of call? How did you respond? Was your decision easy or difficult? Why?

3. Why did God want Isaiah to "make the mind of this people dull, and stop their ears, and shut their eyes"? Doesn't this make his job as a prophet rather difficult?

4. Isaiah asks God of his commission, "How long?" Think about a time when you asked the same question of God. What were the circumstances? Did you get a reply to your question?

Isaiah 7:1–17; 9:1–7 | 4

YHWH and Ahaz

While sitting in class one day during the fall of 1974, my Hebrew instructor remarked that Isaiah 7:9 contained one of the most provocative passages in the Bible for a sermon. The RSV translation seemed anything but exciting to me: "If you will not believe, surely you shall not be established." I guess it lost something in the translation. But that was his point exactly. The English translations often missed the powerful, imaginative spirit of the Hebrew text with its wordplay: *'im lo' ta'amînû kî lo' te'amenû*. John Bright tried to capture the verse with this translation/explanation, "If you do not stand firm—i.e., in trust—you will not be stood firm—i.e., in your position" (Bright, *Authority*, 225). The NRSV seems to reflect his influence in its translation: "If you do not stand firm in faith, you shall not stand at all." I have translated the passage, "If you are not believing, then you will not be living." But it was my instructor's paraphrase that made the verse come alive for me. According to him, YHWH says, "If you won't lean on me, how can I support you?"

In the Old Testament, faith is more a matter of trust than belief. Walter Brueggemann expresses it well when he writes that faith "is not a matter of intellectual content or cognitive belief. It is rather a matter of quite practical reliance upon the assurance of God in a context of risk where one's own resources are not adequate" (Brueggemann, *Isaiah 1–39*, 67). Faith is leaning on God for support in the face of

> **Various translations of Isaiah 7:9b**
>
> "If you do not stand firm in faith, you shall not stand at all." (NRSV)
>
> "If you will not believe, surely you shall not be established." (RSV)
>
> "If you are not believing, then you will not be living." (Author's translation)
>
> "If you won't lean on me, how can I support you?" (Paraphrase)

35

difficult decisions that life thrusts upon us. It is trusting God to be the reliable Giver of our security and our future. Faith makes one vulnerable from the world's point of view because it risks one's self completely, trusting the intangible promises of God, not the material support of the world. Faith, therefore, is not a theoretical exercise in thought as much as it is a vital encounter in life.

Isaiah 7 brings the book of Isaiah to focus on faith through a very specific encounter between YHWH and Ahaz at a particular moment of extreme risk in the life of the nation of Judah. In his commentary, Seitz leads us through the many problems of coordinating the Isaiah account with the parallel account in 2 Kings 16, the general chronology of the kings of Judah and Israel, and what is known through other historical sources. He offers a possible solution by suggesting that Jotham and Ahaz may have shared the throne for a brief period. He rightly cautions, however, that becoming bogged down in historical questions may cause one to miss the point of Isaiah's theological message (Seitz, *Isaiah 1–39*, 61–70). That theological message is clear: Ahaz fails the test of faith in a real-life situation, a national crisis in which his royal position of leadership is threatened.

"Son of No Good"

Ahaz may have just begun his reign as king of Judah, or he may have been the frontrunner in contention for the crown upon Jotham's death. At any rate, he was the responsible leader of Judah's military forces when the two small kingdoms to the north, Israel/Ephraim and Syria/Aram, invaded the land. As the Assyrian forces became active, King Rezin of Syria began enlisting other nations in a defensive coalition to stop them. He was successful in convincing King Pekah of Israel (the Northern Kingdom, also known as Ephraim) to join him, but Ahaz refused to commit the Southern Kingdom, Judah, to the alliance. So Rezin and Pekah joined forces and threatened to invade Judah, depose Ahaz, and place a puppet ruler on the throne who would then add Judah's army to the defensive coalition. Whatever may have been the historical identity of this intended puppet ruler, Isaiah names him "Son of No Good" (Isa. 7:6), a "Ne'er Do Well" or "Good for Nothing."

> "Ahaz was like the man who locked himself in the broom closet because he was afraid that his enemy would come and lock him in the broom closet."

Ahaz's reaction to this threat was fear. Isaiah 7:1 says that the two kings "went up to attack Jerusalem, but could not mount an attack against it." It may be that Ahaz panicked in the face of this invasion and immediately withdrew all his troops from the countryside into Jerusalem, abandoning all of Judah except the capital without engaging in battle. Ahaz was like the man who locked himself in the broom closet because he was afraid that his enemy would come and lock him in the broom closet. Fearful that the war would end in a siege of Jerusalem, Ahaz made the siege of Jerusalem inevitable.

Ahaz was out inspecting the city's water supply one day when YHWH initiated an encounter with the king through the persons of Isaiah and Isaiah's son Shear-jashub. Ahaz evidently had a plan for dealing with the invaders. He had drawn his army into the city of Jerusalem for its defense and their protection. He wanted to guard the principal water supply of the city so that any siege would become a drawn-out affair, and he was ready to send (or perhaps, had already sent) messengers asking for the aid of the Assyrian Empire. Until this time, Judah had been relatively untouched by the Assyrians. They had paid no tribute nor were they a concern to the Assyrian administration. This plan of Ahaz would change everything!

Smoke, but No Fire

YHWH offered Ahaz another plan. The message that Isaiah delivered, "Take heed, be quiet, do not fear, and do not let your heart be faint" (7:4), is *not* the equivalent of "Just relax and everything will be all right." Rather, it is a challenge to take stock in one's situation, one's self, and one's resources. "Think for a minute, don't panic, consider realistically the alternatives before you." YHWH sarcastically calls the "fierce anger" of these two kings nothing more than the smoldering smoke of a campfire that has already been extinguished. There may be smoke, but there is no fire. The words that YHWH has put into the prophet's mouth are even more cutting because they do not allow Pekah, the king of Israel, a name; he is just the "son of Remaliah." Realistically, these two small nations are no threat (7:8–9). Their troops are too few to besiege Jerusalem properly, and their supply lines are stretched too thin for a sustained campaign. YHWH challenges Ahaz to size up the situation and act forcefully and confidently for himself, trusting in the God of Judah to give him victory. Standing firm includes resisting the evil plotted against God's people.

YHWH's encounter with Ahaz takes place through the presence of the prophet Isaiah and his son. It is an encounter initiated by YHWH to give positive assurance and guidance to Ahaz. It does not begin with condemnation, but as an effort to help. YHWH makes it clear that the crisis is an opportunity for gaining strength, if Ahaz will live by faith. Ahaz knew the content of faith. He had been schooled in the divine promises made to the house of David (2 Sam. 7:11–17). At his coronation, Ahaz had repeated God's promises: "I will tell of the decree of the LORD: He said to me, 'You are my son; today I have begotten you. Ask of me, and I will make the nations your heritage, and the ends of the earth your possession. You shall break them with a rod of iron, and dash them in pieces like a potter's vessel'" (Ps. 2:7–9). Ahaz knew the theology, but to him it was all just words. In a crisis in the real world, he wanted something more, something that could be seen and touched. Assyrian iron was easier to trust than YHWH's words.

YHWH was not without a visible sign, however. Shear-jashub was with his father, Isaiah. Everyone knew the name of the prophet's son, which translated as either "It Returns in Pieces" or "A Remnant Shall Return." This name could be heard as a promise or a threat by the king. If Ahaz were to trust YHWH, lead Judah to fight its own battles, and stay away from entanglements with Assyria, then Israel might be destroyed, but Judah would remain as a remnant of the Davidic empire. On the other hand, if Ahaz insisted on following his own plan of purchasing Assyrian protection, then only a remnant of Judah would remain when the smoke cleared. YHWH encountered Ahaz in the visible sign and the spoken word; Ahaz gave them a blind eye and a deaf ear. He refused to lean on YHWH.

> "But he [Ahaz] must believe or he will not be established. He refuses to believe, and the prophet follows with an oracle of judgment against him and his father's house."— Seitz, *Isaiah 1–39*, Interpretation, 78.

Second Chances

"Again the Lord spoke to Ahaz" (7:10). God does not give up on people. This is shown time and time again in scripture. Exodus 3:10–4:17 records an encounter between YHWH and Moses in which YHWH dealt with the objections and excuses of a reluctant shepherd. Jonah 3:1 records the second chance YHWH gave a reluctant prophet. It is a measure of the graciousness of YHWH that a reluctant king is spoken to "again." YHWH's persistence, however, is not simply an expression of grace. Ahaz, as was true of Moses and Jonah, could continue to refuse to respond to YHWH's instruction. The very persistence of God's offer clarifies that the refusal is deliberate and willful, and it expresses the true intent of the one who rejects God's ways. Ahaz could not later say, "It was a mistake. I misunderstood." YHWH's gift of a second chance is a double-edged sword: It does offer a way to obedience, but it also makes disobedience undeniably obvious to all.

The new word from YHWH to Ahaz is an astounding invitation: "Ask any sign you want to of YHWH your God. It can be anything as high as the heavens or as low as the very depths of the earth" (au. trans.). Nothing was withheld from Ahaz. God was that intent upon supporting the king. Even more astounding is the use of the second person pronoun by YHWH. YHWH still claimed to be the God of Ahaz, "YHWH your God" (7:11). All Ahaz had to do was lean upon YHWH. Ahaz, however, turned to Isaiah the prophet with his most pious expression and said, "I would never dream of putting YHWH to the test. Who do you think I am, Gideon? Why,

> "YHWH's gift of a second chance is a double-edged sword: it does offer a way to obedience, but it also makes disobedience undeniably obvious to all."

we learned in Sabbath school what it says in Deuteronomy 6:16: 'Do not put the LORD your God to the test.' Far be it from me to ask for a sign. Why, that would be as if I didn't trust YHWH!" (au. trans.). Of course, the polished halo act does not fool YHWH, Isaiah, or the reader. Ahaz does not want to ask for a sign, even the most impossible heavenly or hellish one, because he is convinced that YHWH indeed would grant it. If it were granted, then Ahaz would have to change his plan. Ahaz could not even tolerate the thought, so he used piety as a cover-up for a lack of faith. Faith, remember, is not so much a *belief* as it is a *trust*, the willingness to lean on YHWH.

Isaiah loses all patience with Ahaz. He stops, for the moment, being the mouthpiece of YHWH and gives the king a piece of his prophetic mind. "Hear then, O house of David! Is it too little for you to weary mortals, that you weary my God also?" (7:13). Ahaz must have been something of a tiresome bore to Isaiah even before this encounter. Now the king has gone too far by using a hypocritical piety before God himself. According to Isaiah's words, such an attitude excludes the king from a personal relationship with God. The prophet says only "my" God, not "our" God or "your" God.

"God with Us"

YHWH would give a sign after all. "Look, the young woman is with child and shall bear a son, and shall name him Immanuel" (7:14). As Christians, we bring a special reverence to this verse. We will discuss that below. But what did this sign mean to Ahaz in his context? YHWH's encounter with Ahaz did not offer an irrelevant answer to the king. It was not "Be patient, Ahaz, and in seven hundred years someone will be born to solve your problem." Within the context of Isaiah, it is as if the prophet points beyond the king toward the queen standing in the background and says, "See over there, she is already pregnant with a son whose name will be 'God with Us.'" For Ahaz and his war, even that sign is not unambiguous because one can "fight with us" either as an ally or as an opponent.

> "Ahaz is called to live in an alternative world governed by this faithful God and by none other."—Walter Brueggemann, *Isaiah 1–39*, Westminster Bible Companion, 68.

Isaiah continues to explain the sign. The prince will be able to enjoy abundance (eating curds and honey) within two or three years because the threatening kingdoms of Syria and Israel will have disappeared (regardless of what policy Ahaz pursues). That should have been the extent of the sign, but because Ahaz refused to lean on YHWH and insisted upon trusting the king of Assyria, there would be no happy ending. Instead, the king, the people, and even the land of Judah would find themselves involved in greater struggles than they had ever imagined (7:17). All the border skirmishes Judah had fought with Ephraim over the previous two centuries would in no way prepare them for what they would face as vassals of the iron-fisted king of Assyria. Ahaz would save his throne, but at the cost of his country's soul.

The sign of Immanuel, "God with Us," did have great significance in the time of Ahaz. Ahaz did have a son, Hezekiah. Within two years, by 732 B.C.E., Syria and Israel had been greatly reduced by the Assyrian Empire. When Hezekiah became king, he was responsible for movements of religious reform and political restoration. As Seitz declares, it was no accident that in 2 Kings 18:7 the Deuteronomistic Historian says of Hezekiah, "God was with him" (Seitz, *Isaiah 1–39*,

70). Nevertheless, the sign of Immanuel is greater than King Hezekiah.

"A Child Has Been Born for Us"

Isaiah 9:2–7 proclaims the birth of a child, the gift of a son, who makes all the difference between God's people living in darkness or in light, between the suffering of defeat and the joy of victory. This birth announced in chapter 9 should be read in connection with the promise of Immanuel in Isaiah 7:14. It is certainly a royal birth, because "authority rests upon his shoulders. . . . His authority shall grow continually, and there shall be endless peace for the throne of David and his kingdom" (9:6b, 7).

This birth announcement might be read as a hopeful description of Hezekiah's birth, because the darkness of the military threat of Syria and Israel did overshadow Judah at that time, and the light of liberation was about to break. That darkness, however, was only the first shadows at twilight compared to the darkness of the Assyrian domination that Judah would suffer. The brief light of Hezekiah's reign would be quickly extinguished by his son and successor, Manasseh. Manasseh would repeal all the religious reforms of Hezekiah and mislead the nation "to do more evil than the nations had done that the LORD destroyed before the people of Israel" (2 Kings 21:9). The hope for a government "with justice and with righteousness from this time onward and forevermore" (Isa. 9:7b) certainly was not fulfilled in the person of Hezekiah. The promise of Immanuel is consistent with Hezekiah but is greater than Hezekiah.

The people who lived in darkness with Assyrian masters through the fifty-seven years of the reigns of Manasseh and Amon may have recalled Isaiah's words about Immanuel, "God with Us," with renewed hope at the coronation of Josiah. The ascension of a new king is like a birth. The coronation ceremony preserved in Psalm 2 declares, "You are my son; today I have begotten you" (Ps. 2:7; see the discussion by Seitz, 86). Josiah did lead the nation in major religious reform and in a sweeping effort of political restoration just as the Assyrian Empire was collapsing. Darkness was lifting and a new light was shining. The Deuteronomistic Historian

> "For a child has been born for us, a son given to us; authority rests upon his shoulders; and he is named Wonderful Counselor, Mighty God, Everlasting Father, Prince of Peace."—Isaiah 9:6

could write of Josiah, "Before him there was no king like him, who turned to the LORD with all his heart, with all his soul, and with all his might, according to all the law of Moses; nor did any like him arise after him" (2 Kings 23:25). But the good, young king died in battle at Megiddo at the hands of the Egyptian Pharaoh Neco. The promise of Immanuel is consistent with Josiah, but is greater than Josiah.

The Isaiah tradition as seen in the whole book of Isaiah reads the promise of Immanuel (7:14), who is also called "Wonderful Counselor, Mighty God, Everlasting Father, Prince of Peace" (9:6), in terms of "the former time" and "the latter time" (9:1). The former time is the eighth century period (B.C.E.) of the Assyrian Empire and Isaiah of Jerusalem. The latter time is the period of return from Babylonian exile and the restoration of Israel promised in Isaiah 40–55. Were there hopes for Immanuel to be revealed at that time? The book of Isaiah preserves this "glorious, celebrative affirmation that Yahweh, through a human Davidic king, will create a wondrous new possibility for Judah that is unqualified and unconditional" (Brueggemann, *Isaiah 1–39*, 82). The book of Isaiah also knows that this affirmation was unfulfilled.

No human figure completely fulfilled all the great hopes poetically expressed in Isaiah 7:14 and 9:2–7 by the time the whole book of Isaiah was completed. Immanuel remained a future hope. Therefore, when a man was troubled by the seeming unfaithfulness of his young bride-to-be, an angel could bring him out of his dark fears by saying, "Emmanuel, God with us" (see Matthew 1:23). Since then, Christianity has separated world history into the former time of B.C. (B.C.E.) and the latter time of A.D. (C.E., or Common Era), and wherever people have found themselves lost in the darkness of sin, they have sung, "O Come, O Come, Emmanuel." The witness of the New Testament is that God's wonderful promise of Immanuel, "God with Us," is at last fulfilled in Jesus, the Christ.

A Multilayered Reading

Brueggemann states that we must admit a "multilayered reading" (*Isaiah 1–39*, 82) of this passage. The legitimate use of these words by the church in its preaching of Christ does not negate, nor should it blind us to, their importance in YHWH's encounter with Ahaz in 734 B.C.E. An understanding of their relevance for Ahaz can, in fact, only help to clarify their continuing importance for the community of faith today as God still challenges us, "If you won't lean on me, how can I support you?"

It is important to note that this "you" is plural. The failure of Ahaz to rely upon YHWH made it impossible for him to function as a fit leader of the people of God. Judah would suffer because of his failure. The consequences for Judah are spelled out in Isaiah 7:18–25 with the four short sayings beginning, "On that day . . ." The fly and bee (vv. 18–19) are pests with bite and sting. Wherever Judah turns, it will be met with hurt. Shaving (v. 20) refers to the practice of humiliating prisoners of war by shaving their head, beard, and genitals ("feet" is a euphemism for the male genitals at several points in the Old Testament, such as Judg. 3:24; 2 Sam. 11:8; Isa. 6:2). The people of Judah will be carried off into exile as humiliated slaves. At first glance, verses 21–22 may seem odd in this series with their promise of honey, curds, and abundance. The meaning, however, is clear because these verses follow the word of exile. The people who are left in the land will be so few that even the meager resources they have (one cow and two sheep) will provide more than enough for their numbers. Finally, verses 23–25 speak of the reversal of the valuable, cultivated land into a harsh land good only for hunting and wild grazing. The lack of faith on the part of the leader of God's people can lead to the destruction of that people.

> "The powerful, visionary poetry of this oracle permits more than one reading. . . . For Christians, the decisive rehearing of the text pertains to Jesus, who is the great light in the darkness. But even that rehearing with reference to Jesus is not exclusive. Alongside that we may entertain many rehearings in which new human agents enact the light that shines in the darkness. The transformative zeal of Yahweh for new peace and prosperity marked by justice and righteousness is undiminished and undeterred."—Walter Brueggemann, *Isaiah 1–39*, Westminster Bible Companion, 85.

In the final analysis, however, the thrust of this event is personal. The encounter between YHWH and Ahaz did not lead to an easy restoration of a personal relationship of trust for Ahaz. Instead, meeting Isaiah and hearing YHWH's word forced Ahaz to make a decision, and his decision effectively ended whatever personal relationship based on faith that may have existed between YHWH and himself. YHWH could expose Ahaz's

 Want to Know More?

About Ahaz? See Paul J. Achtemeier, ed., *HarperCollins Bible Dictionary*, rev. ed., 19.

About the Messianic interpretation of Isaiah 7:14; 9:2–7? See Ronald E. Clements, *Old Testament Prophecy: From Oracles to Canon* (Louisville, Ky.: Westminster John Knox Press, 1996), 56–77.

About the Old Testament concept of faith? See Horst Dietrich Preuss, *Old Testament Theology*, vol. 2, 160–65.

hypocrisy and lack of faith. YHWH could explain the results that the king's lack of faith would cause for Judah. But YHWH could not support Ahaz in the crisis because Ahaz would not lean on YHWH. Judah's tragedy is Ahaz's failure to trust that "God is with us."

? Questions for Reflection

1. Isaiah 7:9 can be paraphrased, "If you won't lean on me, how can I support you?" Have there been times in your life when you heard God say this to you? Have you ever wanted to say this to someone else? What were the circumstances? What did you say?

2. Isaiah 7:10 states, "Again the LORD spoke to Ahaz." Think of another instance from scripture when God gave the people a second chance. What reasons does God have for giving second chances?

3. God tells Ahaz that he can ask any sign of God and it will be granted. Ahaz declines, saying that he would never put God to the test. What is wrong with his answer? Isn't that the way we should respond? Why not?

4. There is a difference of opinion among scholars as to whether the royal birth that is announced in these passages was meant to point to the arrival of Jesus, the Messiah, or the birth of a future king. After reading these passages, what do you think? Does it matter one way or the other?

Isaiah 36–37 | 5

YHWH and Hezekiah

We like proverbs and popular sayings. Furthermore, we believe proverbs are true, even when they are contradictory. "Absence makes the heart grow fonder," but "Out of sight, out of mind," or even more, "When the cat's away, the mice will play." We trust these sayings because they preserve the collective wisdom of the shared experience of our culture. Everyone has had the occasion to say, "Like father, like son." Grandma observes Johnny's misbehavior and says, "He's a chip off the old block." Mary wins a musical competition at school and someone remarks, "The acorn doesn't fall far from the tree." We expect children to be like their parents. But it is not always so. It is not outside our experience to be asked by heartbroken parents, "Where did we go wrong? What did we do wrong?" when their child, who has everything, is arrested for shoplifting. They never acted like that! And there are those cases where a child excels in calculus when her parents can barely balance a checkbook. Where did that DNA come from? What proverb covers the different child?

Isaiah could have used such a proverb, because he had to deal with both Ahaz (Isaiah 7) and his son Hezekiah (Isaiah 36–37). These two kings of Judah could not have been more different in the way they put their faith into practice and in the ways they related to YHWH and his prophet.

Isaiah 36–39 form a literary unit that offers a portrait of Hezekiah. The first two chapters of this literary unit (chaps. 36–37) focus on the king and his willingness to let his faith in YHWH and his trust in the prophet Isaiah shape his political decisions, even in the face of tremendous pressure. From the very beginning, these two chapters invite a comparison of Hezekiah to his father, Ahaz. For his part,

Ahaz had failed to live by faith and refused to request a sign from God (see unit 4). In spite of that refusal, Isaiah announced a prophetic sign: "Behold, the young woman is already pregnant and she will bear a son and will call his name Immanuel. By the time this child is three or four years old, he will be eating royally because these two kings and kingdoms which you fear will be history" (7:14–16, au. trans.). Whatever christological meaning this prophecy holds, for Ahaz and his generation it spoke of Hezekiah and the possibilities his reign would bring. Thus some thirty-two years after the Syro-Ephraimitic War (Isa. 7:1), Judah again faces a crisis: "King Sennacherib of Assyria came up against all the fortified cities of Judah and captured them" (36:1). This crisis of 701 B.C.E. was far more serious than the invasion by the small, overextended forces of Syria and Israel that Ahaz faced in Isaiah 7. Hezekiah faced the brutal army of the Assyrian Empire. Whereas Rezin and Pekah were unable even to engage Judah's forces in combat (7:1), Sennacherib boasts of capturing forty-six fortified cities of Judah and says of Hezekiah, "Himself I made a prisoner in Jerusalem, his royal residence, like a bird in a cage. I surrounded him with earthwork in order to molest those who were leaving his city's gate" (Miller and Hayes, 361). How would Hezekiah respond to the challenge?

> **The Structure of Isaiah 36–37**
> 1. Situation (36:1–3): Only Jerusalem is left
> 2. The Rabshakeh's Speech (36:4–10): A question of trust
> 3. Dramatic Interlude (36:11–12): Request denied
> 4. The Rabshakeh's Speech (36:13–20): Hezekiah is a deceiver
> 5. Delegation Response (36:21–22): Not a word
> 6. Royal Response and Request (37:1–4): Let God answer
> 7. Prophetic Response (37:5–7): Return and Death
> 8. Assyrian Speech (37:8–13): God and king are useless
> 9. Royal Appeal (37:14–20): Thou art God alone
> 10. Prophetic Response (37:21–29): The divine plan will be fulfilled
> 11. Continuation (37:30–35): Sign and promise
> 12. Conclusion (37:36–38): Death in camp and Temple

The Taunting of the Rabshakeh

It is of no small significance that the location of the stories of Isaiah 7 and 36 is the same: "the conduit of the upper pool on the highway to the Fuller's Field" (7:3 and 36:2). For a city under the risk of siege, there is no more important place than the key to its water supply. Vital encounters take place there. The vital decision between doubt and trust is made there. Hezekiah, however, does not encounter the urgings to faith given by Yahweh's prophet as Ahaz did (7:4ff.). He is accosted with the taunting, intimidating speech of his enemy. King Sennacherib had sent his representative, the Rabshakeh, to offer the terms of surrender.

With so much of Judah already devastated, Sennacherib probably felt that his personal presence was not necessary to obtain Hezekiah's surrender. By not being there, Sennacherib further undermined the prestige of Hezekiah. He sent the Rabshakeh, an Assyrian chief officer who functioned either as the chief of staff for the Assyrian forces or who was head of the inner circle of personal advisors surrounding the king. If the Assyrian king would not be present, Hezekiah would not be humiliated by attending the discussion. So he sent a delegation to hold talks with the Rabshakeh. There were, however, no negotiations. The Assyrian demand was clear, and as far as Sennacherib could determine, Hezekiah's acceptance was a foregone conclusion.

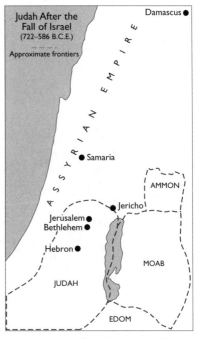

Judah after the Fall of Israel

Assyrian swagger and pride filled the words of the Rabshakeh, which were intended to further demoralize and humiliate Jerusalem's defenders. "Thus says the great king, the king of Assyria" in verse 4 magnifies the power and majesty of Sennacherib, whose name is not invoked out of awesome respect. These words stand in marked contrast to the Rabshakeh's references to Hezekiah, whom he routinely calls by name and to whom he gives no title at all. With the Rabshakeh as spokesman, the king of Assyria demands to know who could grant Hezekiah such security that he would dare rebel against Assyria. Notice how often the verb "rely" appears in this speech of the Rabshakeh. The object of the trust, confidence, and faith of Hezekiah and his people is the main issue. The Rabshakeh wanted to convince the people that all grounds of confidence were insufficient. Any strategy of war that Judah had was only fanciful, empty words.

Do they rely on Egypt's promises of aid? If so, they will be disappointed. The Rabshakeh warns them that such words are false and dangerous. Egypt is like a cane with an unnoticed crack in it. If you

47

lean on it, not only does it break, but its splinters pierce your hand. That was no real news to Hezekiah and Judah. Isaiah had already warned that "Egypt's help is worthless and empty" (30:7), and had prophesied ruin if Hezekiah trusted in Egypt (31:3). But it was only the beginning of the Rabshakeh's speech.

The Rabshakeh declares that if the words that Judah relied on were YHWH's promises, then these too were empty. It is somewhat surprising to hear the name YHWH on the lips of a non-Israelite. Nevertheless, the Rabshakeh uses the divine name in verse 7 and again in verse 10. These uses of the personal name of God by one who does not truly know YHWH add emphasis to the issue of trust and make the blasphemy of the Assyrian officer even more evident (see Preuss, *Old Testament Theology*, vol. 2, 165–66). The Assyrian claims that trust in YHWH is misplaced because YHWH could no longer be relied upon since Hezekiah's religious reform limited the worship of YHWH to the one altar in the temple in Jerusalem. According to this polytheistic way of thinking, either YHWH's powers were limited now that the number of altars of worship had been limited, or YHWH refused to help because he is angry with Hezekiah for this downsizing of Israel's worship, and therefore YHWH's glory. These words must have struck a responsive chord within some Judeans. This same type of thinking is expressed in Jeremiah 44:15–18, in which they point out that things were better before temple reforms than after them! Playing upon the fears and tensions brought about by religious change, the Rabshakeh fosters doubt in YHWH's ability or willingness to help. "The stakes are awfully great at this juncture," writes Seitz. "Shall we trust the 'Thus says the Lord' of Isaiah or the 'Thus says the great king' of the Rabshakeh?" (Seitz, 246).

"He [Sennacharib] is requesting (and anticipating) surrender of Hezekiah. . . . The dramatic affect achieved thereby is enormous: the bulk of the account now focuses on the speeches of the Assyrian Rabshakeh, as he sues for surrender and, getting no response (37:21), must dig himself deeper and deeper into a position of blasphemous disrespect."—Seitz, *Isaiah 1–39*, Interpretation, 245–46.

Resistance is Futile

The Rabshakeh points out that if Hezekiah's war strategy was based on Judah's own resources, then all was lost because such war plans were merely words written on paper. He does this in dramatic, taunting fashion. With magnificent bravado before all the people of Jerusalem who were on the wall to observe the event, the Rabshakeh offers two thousand horses to Hezekiah to use in battle against the Assyrians, if only Hezekiah could prove he had sufficient and trained cavalrymen to use them. Of course Hezekiah had no such human resources. The Assyrian's point was made. Surely Judah did not trust in its own resources; they were unable to "repulse a single captain among the least" of the Assyrian forces (v. 9). Further resistance was futile.

The Rabshakeh concludes his first speech with one final, daring declaration that YHWH himself had given the orders to Sennacherib to go and destroy Jerusalem! Assyrian intelligence must have done its work well. Not only was it aware of Hezekiah's religious reforms and able to exploit them, but the empire also knew enough of Isaiah's preaching to use it for their benefit. Isaiah had indeed prophesied that YHWH said, "Ah, Assyria, the rod of my anger—the club in their hands is my fury! Against a godless nation I send him, and against the people of my wrath I command him, to take spoil and seize plunder, and to tread them down like the mire of the streets" (10:5–6). YHWH did use Assyria as his instrument of judgment upon Judah, but that does not mean that Assyria was an obedient servant of YHWH. The Rabshakeh could use theology in his propaganda, but his true attitude toward YHWH is revealed in his later speeches in which he denies the uniqueness and power of YHWH. He compares YHWH to the gods of other nations. Their failures, he asserts, should convince Judah that YHWH will also prove to be impotent against Assyria (36:18–20). In his attempt to intimidate Hezekiah into surrender, the Rabshakeh only proves the rest of Isaiah's preaching about Assyria: "Shall the ax vaunt itself over the one who wields it, or the saw magnify itself against the one who handles it? . . . The glory of his forest and his fruitful land the LORD will destroy, both soul and body" (10:15, 18). Even so, the Rabshakeh's speech is effective as rhetoric of intimidation.

The delegation's reply to this first speech of the Rabshakeh is less a direct response than it is an attempt to manage the crisis the speech was creating. The leaders appeal to the Rabshakeh to use the diplomatic language of Aramaic so the Hebrew-speaking public will not be able to understand the talks, which they sense are not going well for their side. It seems to be a case of "what you don't know can't hurt you." One way to deal with a crisis is to ignore it in the hopes that it will go away. These leaders hope that the crisis can be contained through a cover-up. If the public is uninformed, then the crisis management team's job becomes easier.

The Rabshakeh, however, senses the delegation's discomfort and

49

its inability to respond to his challenges. He immediately presses his advantage with a second speech, addressed directly to the people. After all, they would share in the consequences of continued resistance (v. 12). The speech, in Hebrew, calls into question the reliability of Hezekiah's leadership. In verse 14, the Rabshakeh sows doubt about Hezekiah's statesmanship, and in verse 15 he plants doubts about Hezekiah's theology. Verses 16–17 tear at the solidarity of the city as the Rabshakeh urges the people to act independently for their own sake. He seems to be saying that surrender is all that is necessary to return life to normal. Afterward, the people could eat and drink just as they had always done, for a while. Even the exile that Sennacherib had already planned for Judah is presented softly. It would be to "a land like your own land, a land of grain and wine, a land of bread and vineyards" (v. 17). It would not, however, be "a land flowing with milk and honey" (Ex. 3:8). The land of Sennacherib's promise could not match the land of YHWH's promise.

> "When the Assyrian insists on speaking Hebrew, the language of Judah, which everyone understands, and moreover speaking it in a 'loud voice' (v. 13) for everyone to hear, we can enjoy anticipating the spectacle of him being humiliated later in full view of the citizens of Jerusalem."—John F. A. Sawyer, *Isaiah*, vol. 2, Daily Study Bible, 24.

"Thus Says the King"

Sennacherib cannot replace YHWH. The Rabshakeh's speeches have hinted that the Assyrian attitude places the king above YHWH. The speeches begin, "Thus says the great king, the king of Assyria . . ." (36:4), and "Hear the words of the great king, the king of Assyria! Thus says the king . . ." (36:13–14). These grand introductions may be read as challenges to the prophetic declaration, "Thus says YHWH . . ." The Assyrian demand assumes that YHWH is no different from the local deities of other conquered nations. Sennacherib clearly feels superior to YHWH. "Who among all the gods of these countries have saved their countries out of my hand, that the LORD should save Jerusalem out of my hand?" (36:20).

The people do not answer the Assyrian's question. The king has ordered their silence, and they obediently wait for his response. Hezekiah hears the delegation's report and joins them in the tearing of garments as a sign of anguish and distress before YHWH. Unlike Ahaz before him, Hezekiah seeks Isaiah's input. He sends the delegation to inform Isaiah of these events and to ask the prophet to pray. Surprisingly, there is no record of a prayer by the prophet. Instead, the prophet has an immediate word from YHWH assuring the king that the Assyrian threat will be dealt with adequately (37:6–7). Sennacherib will die violently in Assyria (37:7).

In the meantime, the Rabshakeh returns to Lachish only to find that Sennacherib has left there to engage Ethiopian (Egyptian) forces, which were under the leadership of Tirhakah. This army will be defeated. It will not be the Egyptians who deliver Jerusalem from danger. In fact, Sennacherib, while meeting the Egyptian challenge, still takes time to send a letter to Hezekiah with a third demand for Jerusalem's unconditional surrender. The letter is an attack upon YHWH. "Do not let your God on whom you rely deceive you" (37:10). In spite of Isaiah's oracle, the Assyrian threat continues. Hezekiah holds it in his own hands! How will he respond?

Hezekiah's Prayer

Hezekiah's response is presented in dramatic fashion. One can almost see the king immediately going to the temple, spreading the letter out on the floor, and saying, "Here, Lord, read this!" The response is as personal as it is immediate. There is no thought of concealing the facts, and there is no appeal to a second party. Hezekiah himself goes before YHWH and offers a personal prayer. Whereas Ahaz avoided God's input, Hezekiah seeks God's presence. The prayer of Hezekiah is easily divided into three sections: doxology (v. 16), complaint (vv. 17–19), and petition (v. 20) (Brueggemann, *Isaiah 1–39*, 292–94). The doxology offers significant titles of YHWH besides the "God of Israel." He is "YHWH of armies," one who has all power at his command. He is "enthroned above the cherubim," a phrase that calls attention to YHWH as the God of Israel, but one also recognizes YHWH's special presence without limiting YHWH

> Walter Brueggemann identifies four themes in this passage that serve the larger purpose of the book of Isaiah:
> 1. *Zion theology:* The well-being of the city of Jerusalem is a core preoccupation of this tradition;
> 2. *Faith:* The ability and willingness to trust in YHWH in situations of risk is a key theme of Isaiah;
> 3. *Isaiah:* The prophet is a key player in this passage.
> 4. *King Hezekiah:* He is presented as "the good king who trusts" as opposed to his father, King Ahaz, "the bad king who fears."
>
> —Adapted from *Isaiah 1–39*, Westminster Bible Companion, 284.

as a "localized" deity. YHWH is significantly the creator of the heavens and the earth, therefore YHWH is the only God of "all the kingdoms of the earth.".

The central section of the prayer is a complaint. This communal complaint offered by the king in a time of national crises is different than a lament. A lament assesses a dismal situation that is already accomplished and, from a practical standpoint, from where there is no hope of rescue or reconstruction. A complaint, on the other hand, "was articulated when the final blow had not yet fallen, when there still was time to argue a case before YHWH" (Gerstenberger, *Psalms*, part 1, 11.) It addresses YHWH with the expectation that YHWH is able to see, evaluate, and act to redeem the situation. The facts of Sennacherib's letter are not discounted. The assertions of previous conquests are disconcerting because they are true (vv. 18–19)! But the maker of the complaint dares to make a petition (v. 20) based not on himself or the situation, but on the unique character of YHWH, who will protect the sanctity of YHWH's holy name and enable YHWH's purposes among the nations to be fulfilled.

Following Hezekiah's prayer, the prophet Isaiah appears with an assurance that God has heard the king's prayer and will respond positively to it. In fact, it is "because you have prayed to me concerning King Sennacherib of Assyria" (v. 21) that YHWH is acting. YHWH's response to the prayer may be divided into three sections that roughly parallel the three discourses of Sennacherib toward Hezekiah, namely, 37:22–29, 30–32, and 33–35. The response is followed by the recital of the fulfillment of YHWH's word to Hezekiah.

Pride Goeth Before a Fall

Just as the first speech of the Rabshakeh is Sennacherib's address to Hezekiah, the first section of Isaiah's oracle to Hezekiah is YHWH's address to Sennacherib. Sennacherib is accused of mocking YHWH, the "Holy One of Israel," in his prideful speech and haughty actions against Judah (v. 23). The six (a less than perfect number) first-person pronouns used by Sennacherib in verses 24–25 are evidence enough of his arrogance. But we know the proverb "Pride goeth before a fall." Sennacherib's "I's" are countered by the first-person speech of YHWH in verses 26–29. The "I" of YHWH overpowers the "I" of Sennacherib. YHWH's response provides a definitive answer to the Rabshakeh's mocking questions to Hezekiah in 36:4–5:

"On what do you base this confidence of yours? . . . On whom do you now rely?" Hezekiah relied upon YHWH.

Just as the Rabshakeh's second speech is addressed to the people listening on the wall, YHWH's second discourse concerns the people of Judah. The "you" of verse 30 is singular and seems to refer to Hezekiah, whom YHWH offers a sign promising limited destruction. Nevertheless, the imperatives of that verse are plurals and therefore refer to the population in general. Verses 31–32 refer unambiguously to the people. The people of Jerusalem will be unable to plant and harvest as normal in the first year following the Assyrian crisis, and the second year will not be much better. The sign is that by the third year, things will be back to normal. This is good news to all.

> "The blasphemous words of Sennacherib and his officials are rebuked, and the theological point the narrative wishes to make is made: Jerusalem is saved from the hand of Sennacherib so that all the kingdoms on earth might know that Yahweh is God alone."—Seitz, *Isaiah 1–39*, 253.

The third discourse of Sennacherib is a letter directed to Hezekiah. It warns the king not to be deceived by YHWH's promise that Jerusalem will not be captured. Sennacherib points out that he has utterly destroyed other lands and assures Hezekiah that he will do the same to Jerusalem and its king. The third section of YHWH's response is to take up such a challenge directly. YHWH promises that Sennacherib "shall not come into this city" or even "shoot an arrow there" (v. 33). The city will be defended and saved by YHWH, not only for the sake of YHWH's promise, but also for the sake of YHWH's own person and honor (v. 35). Sennacherib was wrong. He would go home by the same road that brought him to Jerusalem, and he would do so without victory.

The editorial comment at the end is surprisingly brief. One verse (v. 36) asserts that 185,000 Assyrians died through YHWH's agency. The fact is simply stated. No details are given; none are needed. Then the ultimate fate of Sennacherib is related. He was at home in Nineveh, worshiping his god in a temple, when he was assassinated by his own sons (vv. 37–38). One Assyrian historian adds an intriguing detail. It seems that the very idol statues of the protective gods of the Assyrian king were used as the murder

 Want to Know More?

About Sennacherib? See J. Maxwell Miller and John H. Hayes, *A History of Ancient Israel and Judah* (Louisville, Ky.: Westminster John Knox Press, 1986), 360–61.

About Hezekiah? See Paul J. Achtemeier, ed., *HarperCollins Bible Dictionary*, rev. ed., 420–21.

weapons that killed him (Kaiser, *Isaiah 13–39*, 391). The editor does not mention that Sennacherib's death occurred some twenty years after his assault on Jerusalem. There was no real need to express the timing. It is enough that Isaiah's prophecy of 37:7 had been fulfilled. "The blasphemous words of Sennacherib and his officials are rebuked, and the theological point the narrative wishes to make is made: Jerusalem is saved from the hand of Sennacherib so that all kingdoms on earth might know that Yahweh is God alone" (Seitz, 253).

YHWH was faithful in his promises to Hezekiah, just as Hezekiah had been faithful to YHWH.

? Questions for Reflection

1. The Rabshakeh's taunting points to a key decision that the people must make—should they trust the word of the Lord or the word of the king? Can you name other instances in scripture where the people were faced with this choice? How did they choose? What was the outcome?

2. The constant attacks on YHWH by Sennacherib and the Rabshakeh finally wear Hezekiah down, and he goes to the Lord in prayer (37:16–20). The Lord immediately responds through the words of the prophet Isaiah. Think of a time in your life when you prayed for God's intercession and received an immediate response. Who or what was the "prophet" who delivered the response? How did you feel after receiving the response?

3. Compare the stories of YHWH and Ahaz (unit 4) and YHWH and Hezekiah (unit 5), and discuss the lessons they hold for us about faithfulness to God.

4. It must have been difficult for Hezekiah not to respond in kind to the ceaseless taunting of the Rabshakeh. Have you ever been in a similar situation? How did you respond? What was the outcome?

YHWH and the People, Part Two

I was about nine years old when I rode my bicycle to the Strand Theater in Marietta, Georgia, to see the movie *Gone With the Wind*. My mother was surprised when I walked back into the house a couple of hours later. "Why are you home so soon?" she asked. "I thought that you rode your bike to the movie." I told her that I had, and that the movie had been over for a long time. She questioned me a little more before she began laughing softly. I thought that the movie had ended. The Yankees had burned Atlanta, Scarlett had been on her knees in the dirt swearing that she would never be hungry again, and everyone in the theater had stood up when the lights went on. I did not see what else could happen. Besides that, on the screen there appeared what I thought must have been a fancy word for "The End": INTERMISSION. As far as I was concerned, it was over. I went home. It would be years before I would see the second half of one of the greatest movies ever filmed.

There was a long intermission between Isaiah 39 and Isaiah 40. As far as some were concerned, the relationship between YHWH and the covenant community was over. After the destruction of Jerusalem and the experience of exile in Babylonia, what else was left to happen? It was a 150-year period that Brueggemann has called a "God-muted time" (Brueggemann, *Isaiah 40–66*, 15). It seemed that Isaiah 39 spelled "The End" (especially v. 6). Isaiah 40, however, sounds the theme of the beginning of a new chapter in the relationship between the covenant people and YHWH.

One might conclude that the theme of Isaiah 40:1–11 has to do with the word of YHWH. After all, verse 8 declares, "The grass withers, the flower fades; but the word of our God will stand forever."

While the passage makes significant statements about the word of YHWH, it does so in the context of the intent, impact, and influence that this word has upon the community of faith. One might conclude that the theme of this passage is that of YHWH and prophet. It does seem to be another case of the commissioning of one who is mysteriously present in the heavenly council. The prophet, like Isaiah in chapter 6, hears and responds. Nevertheless, this prophet remains nameless and completely identifies himself with the people. The prophet's story is the people's story, and the prophet's work (v. 6) becomes the people's work (v. 9). Therefore, this is the story of the relationship between YHWH and the covenant people, part two.

> "This tie between Second Isaiah's message of pardon and the theme of divine forgiveness is of fundamental significance in biblical faith."—Paul D. Hanson, *Isaiah 40–66,* Interpretation, 19.

The Heavenly Council

The story begins in the heavenly council. What has happened to Jerusalem has not gone unnoticed by YHWH. God takes the initiative, calling on the heavenly council to comfort the covenant community, which YHWH still claims as "my people" (v. 1). Setting the story first in the heavenly council is a biblical declaration that what will happen to the covenant people is not an accidental, human decision. YHWH alone determines, and all the resources of the universe are involved in the fulfillment of the divine will. As Paul Hanson points out, "The realms that serve God reach far beyond human ken" (*Isaiah 40–66,* 17). Far from being a forgotten group of exiles in Babylon, the covenant community is the hot topic at the command center of the universe! Heaven is about to change the shape of Earth's current events.

YHWH gives a plural command, "[All of you] comfort my people." It is also a double command, "Comfort, O comfort my people." The repetition emphasizes the urgency of the command, just as the prophet emphasizes the commands "Awake, awake" (51:9) and "Rouse yourself, rouse yourself!" (51:17). Comforting is an urgent task, for this comfort is not simply an expression of sympathy: "There, there, don't cry, things will get better. I am sure everything will work out all right. Until then, you have my condolences. I'm sorry that everything is so rough." The Hebrew concept of comfort, *nhm,* includes both the emotion of compassion and the activity of bringing relief. In Lamentations 1:7 and 9 "comfort" and "help" are parallel terms with regard to Jerusalem: "When her people fell into the hand of the foe and there was no one to help her . . . her downfall was appalling, with none to comfort her." Isaiah 51:3 makes the connection between compassionate feeling and helping activity explicit: "The Lord will surely comfort [*nḥm*] Zion and will look with compassion [*nḥm*] on all her ruins; he will make her deserts like Eden" (NIV). Whereas the great crisis of exile had led some biblical writers to lament that God's people had no one to comfort them in their oppression (see Eccl. 4:1 as well as Lam.1:2, 9, 17, and 21), Second Isaiah had a vision of God's determination to comfort, relieve, and restore the people of Judah.

God calls on the heavenly powers to "speak tenderly to Jerusalem" (v. 2). Literally, the phrase is the tenderly romantic phrase, "Speak unto the heart" (cf. Gen. 34:3; Judg. 19:3; Ruth 2:13; and Hos. 2:14), which came to have the general sense of uplifting encouragement or reassurance (see Gen. 50:21; 2 Sam. 19:8 [19:7 Eng.]; 2 Chron. 30:22; 32:6). This encouraging proclamation has the specific purpose of announcing the pardon of Judah freely given by YHWH. It is, however, a troubling proclamation, open to various readings, that says "that she has served her term, that her penalty is paid, that she has received from the LORD's hand double for all her sins" (v. 2).

Could it be that sin carries a particular sentence that can be served by a person or a nation, which, once completed, cancels out the sin? Does the prophet say that Judah suffered enough to make God recognize that the people had made up for their faults and deserved once more a full relationship before YHWH? In fact, does the prophet complain that the Heavenly Accountant has not been paying close attention to Judah and therefore YHWH overcharged the covenant people, forcing them to pay twice what their sin was worth? While such a reading may be possible, it certainly is not satisfying nor is it consistent with Second Isaiah's understanding of grace and forgiveness.

"Her Iniquity is Pardoned"

Perhaps the reading of the RSV (including the note) is to be preferred: "Cry to her that her time of service is ended, that her iniquity is pardoned, that she has received from the LORD's hand double for all her sins." The covenant people had suffered grievously at the hands of Assyria and Babylon. There can be no denial of the facts. The people of Israel had experienced a "time of service" like conscripts in military service or those undergoing a period of forced labor. Israel was familiar with such suffering in its history: the people had slaved away in Egypt (Ex. 1:11–14), and common citizens had experienced "hard labor" under Solomon (1 Kings 12:4). The parallelism of Isaiah 40:2 makes it clear that the time of service is connected with iniquity and sin. The fact that the time of service has ended is therefore connected with pardon. The focus of the message is not the people's serving out a sentence, but it is YHWH's forgiveness. As Hanson writes, "This tie between Second Isaiah's message of pardon and the theme of divine forgiveness is of fundamental significance in biblical faith" (*Isaiah 40–66*, 19).

> **What was the Exile?**
> Accounts vary as to exactly how many people were affected by the period known as the exile, but in general this term refers to the period in the sixth century B.C.E. during which part of the population of Judah was deported into Babylonia under King Nebuchadnezzar. Jeremiah lists a total of 4,600 people being deported, while 2 Kings has the number at more than 10,000. In 539 the Babylonian forces were defeated by a combined army of Medes and Persians, and those in exile were free to return home.

The two translations, "Her iniquity is pardoned" and "Her penalty is paid," are not mutually exclusive. The Hebrew word *'awon* may be translated "iniquity" or "guilt," but it carries with it the idea of "punishment for guilt" as well in certain passages (see Isa. 5:18 and Gen. 4:13). The Hebrew term translated "pardoned" or "paid" is a form of the verb *raṣah* meaning "to be accepted (as paid)." The situation is similar to that of the servant in Jesus' parable found in Matthew 18:23–35. In the parable, the slave owes the king 10,000 talents. The amount is unbelievably huge. A free man working for an average daily wage would not earn 10,000 talents in 150,000 years! As Thomas Long has written, "An Egyptian pharaoh couldn't come up with ten thousand talents, much less a slave" (Long, *Matthew*, 211). Even though he could never have paid the debt, the servant pleaded, "Have patience with me, and I will pay you." The king had compassion upon him and forgave him the debt. In Isaiah 40:1–2, YHWH has compassion on the covenant people and pardons their debt. The penalty is counted as satisfied not because of a calculated amount of the people's suffering, but because of God's incalculable grace.

The words declaring that Jerusalem "has received from the LORD's hand double for all her sins" are not a protest on the lips of the prophet. They make up part of the comforting message that YHWH wants proclaimed to "Jerusalem," a symbol of the whole community of faith. The "comfort" that is offered requires a recognition on the part of the community of faith that its current condition is due to its own sinful behavior. The "new" message of Second Isaiah stands on the shoulders of the "old" message of Isaiah of Jerusalem and other eighth century (B.C.E.) prophets who preached judgment (e.g., Amos, Hosea, Micah). The change is God's decision and is not the result of Israel's activity, not even its suffering.

Certainly there is no indication that Jerusalem has paid more than it should have to compensate for its misdeeds. The sins of YHWH's people are not simply particular crimes enacted here and there. The sin of Israel is rebellion (Isa. 1:2). Sin is an attitude that breaks off the personal relationship between YHWH and the individual or nation. It is a rupture that is not automatically resumed after a determined amount of penance is paid. Sinners may "pay for" their sin by suffering twice as much as they ever thought they would, or ten times as much, or even 100 times as much as they ever believed possible. They can never, however, "pay off" their sins in full because sin is not an objective misdeed for which one may offer compensation. Therefore, connecting the "double" of Isaiah 40:2 with the legal tradition of Exodus 22, in which the thief must pay "double," is doubtful. Isaiah is not speaking of a mathematical or economical calculation (or miscalculation) on YHWH's part.

Some see a connection between this "double" in Isaiah 40:2 and the special accountability of Israel as the elect people of YHWH, which is described in Amos 3:2. However, it seems best to understand the phrase in Isaiah 40 as a lively, figurative Hebrew expression which means that Israel had indeed undergone a tremendous amount of suffering due to its sin. Moreover, it may indicate that the nation has arrived at the point at which "the people are no longer able to sustain the burden of their grievous fate" (Westermann, *Isaiah 40–66*, 36). At this point, YHWH freely chooses to act with forgiveness. The comfort in the message of Second Isaiah, as James Smart has pointed out, is "that both in judgment and in mercy God gives full measure flowing over" (Smart, *History and Theology in Second Isaiah*, 45). If the people of God experienced double judgment, they are about to experience a double portion of YHWH's grace.

A Highway for Our God

With verse 3, another, unidentified, voice speaks. Having heard YHWH's decision to comfort the covenant people, it calls for a response from the (other?) heavenly powers to get the activity under-way. The comfort for Jerusalem will not be human condolences, but it will be the helpful presence of God. The heavenly council hears a call to build Interstate 777 for YHWH's triumphal procession into Jerusalem. In Babylon and throughout the ancient Near East, it was a common practice to prepare a highway for the return of a victori-ous king or for a religious procession of a nation's gods at festival cel-ebrations. This "highway for our God" is to be prepared in the wild desert that lies between Babylon and Jerusalem. Where the way encounters mountains, they are to be leveled. Where there are low places, bridges are to be built. Its surface is to be level and smooth, and its design is to be straight. The comforting of Jerusalem will be through the very presence of YHWH and the terms for the con-struction of YHWH's highway indicate that nothing at all will hin-der the gracious entrance of Jerusalem's God.

The prophet speaks of that entrance procession in verse 5: "Thus shall the glory of the LORD be revealed and all mankind together shall see it" (NEB, lit. "all flesh"). The "glory" of YHWH is God's *kabôd,* that is, God's "weighty" presence, which commands a recognition of God's authority to rule. The vision of Second Isaiah extends the per-ception of God's glory to all humankind. What will the people see? What will serve as the physical representation of YHWH's glory on that highway if there are no graven images and no idols made of YHWH?

The prophet leaves that question unanswered for the moment because another voice interrupts the action of the heavenly council in verse 6. Is this YHWH's voice? Verse 5 ended with the assurance that the instructions of verses 4 and 5 had come from the mouth of YHWH. If it is YHWH's voice, then the commissioning of the unnamed prophet we call Second Isaiah has yet another parallel to the commissioning of the Isaiah of Jerusalem in chapter 6. YHWH, or an authorized agent within the heavenly council, commands, "Cry out!" The commission is to call out, to proclaim, to preach.

This prophet, however, exhibits no "Here am I, send me!" spirit. His spirit is the same as the people who at this moment are still in exile, languishing and lamenting, unaware of any heavenly council meeting. They are saying, "Our

"How could we sing the LORD's song in a foreign land?"—Psalm 137:4.

bones are dried up, and our hope is lost; we are cut off completely" (Ezek. 37:11). They are seated by the rivers of Babylon weeping among the willows while their tormentors mock them asking for the songs of Zion. They cry, "How could we sing the LORD's song in a foreign land?" (see Ps. 137:1–4). The prophet asks the commissioning God, "Why bother? What words are there that could make a difference? All the people are grass, their constancy is like the flower of the field. The grass withers, the flower fades when the breath of the LORD blows upon it. What's the use?" God had said, "Preach!" The prophet responded with a despairing question, "What's the use of preaching? Who's going to listen? Do you really think a sermon will make any difference now?"

The Word Stands Forever

Second Isaiah, like Moses (Exodus 3–4), finds out that YHWH takes seriously any questions and objections to the divine call. Just as YHWH answered the complaints of Jeremiah with a challenge to trust (Jer. 15:19–21), so the pessimism of Second Isaiah is challenged in chorus by the whole heavenly council, who cried, "Yes, 'the grass withers, the flower fades; but the word of our God will stand forever'" (v. 8). This verse contains the central truth that Second Isaiah needed to hear in order to overcome the despair of his age and accept the commission to proclaim comfort to YHWH's people.

Admittedly, the human situation is indeed temporary and transitory. Death and decay, failure and suffering are all a part of human existence. But the "word of YHWH" originates beyond the human realm. It is abiding, it is permanent, it is sure. The people of God may have lost land, king, and temple, but they were being offered what could never be taken away, the word of YHWH. It was an invitation to a new beginning that was too wonderful to pass up. The prophet leaves the heavenly council with a new commission and a new message.

Hanson's suggestion that verses 9–11 belong to the prophet (*Isaiah 40–66*, 23) is thought provoking. The prophet calls his people to lift up their voices with his. His work becomes their work.

> "The prophet's initial response to the awesome spectacle of the divine assembly resembles that of Isaiah of Jerusalem (Isaiah 6:5). . . . People of faith from Moses on have responded to an awareness of God's presence with this dread sense of unworthiness and nothingness."—Paul D. Hanson, *Isaiah 40–66*, Interpretation, 23.

One element of the comfort that YHWH brings to the covenant people is their meaningful involvement in the divine plan. The people receive YHWH's comfort when, by faith, they participate in a purpose greater than their own. Zion/Jerusalem is to become an evangelist, unafraid and proclaiming the message, "Here is your God!"

Second Isaiah calls for the people who are still in exile to join with him in proclaiming the good news of the presence of YHWH. The hope of Isaiah 7 is the hope of Isaiah 40, "God is with us, Immanuel!" Everyone who will may see YHWH's glorious presence on the desert highway that will be constructed for the divine processional. There will be no graven images carried on the backs of beasts of burden. There will be no idols lifted by human hands. What, then, will evangelist Jerusalem's words signal when she proclaims, "See, the Lord GOD comes" (v. 10)? The glory of the invisible God will be revealed in the sight of the liberated captives returning home by that desert road. What had been promised in 40:5 is now explained more fully. What YHWH does for the covenant people will have its effect written upon human history. The liberation of the covenant people from the Babylonian captivity will give hope to all the oppressed people of the world that there is indeed one God who "comes with might" and whose "arm rules" (v. 10). Genesis 12:3 will find fulfillment: "In you all the families of the earth shall be blessed."

No Easy Faith

The prophet's call for his people to join with him in the proclamation of the good news from the heavenly council meeting is a call to faith. It is a call for a demonstration not only of a faith that defies the Babylonian claim of supremacy, which gave no thought to the power or presence of YHWH, but also of a faith that overcomes the despair of the covenant people, who had interpreted their misery as proof of YHWH's absence. Their acceptance of the prophetic challenge would prove that "both imperial arrogance and exilic despair are countered. Yahweh is present, powerful, active; Yahweh's presence changes everything" (Brueggemann, *Isaiah 40–66*, 21). Because the prophet challenges the people to proclaim this message while they are still in Babylon, it is a call to a faith that overcomes fear and is ready to redefine its concepts of community and service.

Such faith is not easy. Hanson points to two doubts "that perennially afflict those enduring grievous suffering, the one questioning God's power to change the situation, the other calling into question God's goodness and love" (Hanson, *Isaiah 40–66*, 24–25). The message that Second Isaiah calls on the covenant community to share is one that assures the hearer of YHWH's ability and willingness to act on behalf of the people of faith. The first part of the message (v. 10) is a proclamation of the majestic power of YHWH. Like a divine warrior, YHWH "comes with might." The ruling "arm" of YHWH functions as an expression not simply of power, but emphasizes the idea of the personal exercise of power. YHWH is the mighty, victorious King marching into the city with the booty of conquest. The "reward" and the "recompense" marching before this King will be YHWH's own people coming home once more.

The King is also a Shepherd (v. 11). The change of image is not as radical as it might first appear to the modern reader. While we do not often read the twenty-third Psalm and "The LORD is my shepherd . . ." as a reminder of the kingship of God, the ancient Near East often gave the king the title "shepherd of

 Want to Know More?

About the exile? See John Bright, *A History of Israel*, 4th ed. (Louisville, Ky.: Westminster John Knox Press, 2000), chap. 9.

his people" (Smart, *History and Theology in Second Isaiah*, 53). The conquering King, therefore, is a gentle King. YHWH's sovereignty over the covenant people is not expressed as control over a huge mass of people. Rather, it finds expression in the tender care that YHWH provides to each individual. "The shepherd knows how to make the way easy for every single one" (Westermann, *Isaiah 40–66*, 46). The loving care of the Shepherd for the flock includes carrying the weakest and paying special attention not to overtax those with young. Sheep without a shepherd are lost without hope for survival (Ezek. 34:5; Matt. 9:36). The good news is that God's people have a Shepherd; YHWH is present with the covenant people.

The curtain has risen again. The story is not over. After a long intermission, YHWH is about to do a "new thing."

? Questions for Reflection

1. Discuss the possible interpretations of verse 2. Does it mean that there is a particular sentence that, once served, cancels out the sin? Or that the people had to suffer twice as much as they deserved? Or is there another interpretation that fits better with God's gracious nature?

2. The response to the call for a "highway for our God" is less than enthusiastic. What is going on in the life of the people to make them respond this way?

3. Have you ever been called on to "prepare the way of the Lord" when your life was in a less than perfect state? How did you respond? Why is it so difficult to cry "Here I am, send me!" when our lives feel like they're falling apart?

4. What scriptural passage comes to mind when you read verse 11? Have you thought of God with this imagery before?

From Isaiah 42, 49, 50, 52-53 | 7

YHWH and the Servant

In Acts 8:31, an Ethiopian eunuch invites Philip to join him in his chariot for Bible study. "Now the passage of the scripture that he was reading was this: 'Like a sheep he was led to the slaughter, and like a lamb silent before its shearer, so he does not open his mouth. In his humiliation justice was denied him. Who can describe his generation? For his life is taken away from the earth'" (Acts 8:32–33). The eunuch then asks Philip an important question, "About whom . . . does the prophet say this, about himself or about someone else?" Philip's answer is to start with this scripture about YHWH's Suffering Servant and share with him the good news of Jesus (Acts 8:35).

According to the New Testament (see also Matt. 12:17–21), Jesus is the Servant described in the so-called Servant Songs of Second Isaiah **(Isa. 42:1–9; 49:1–13; 50:4–9; and 52:13–53:12).** Is that right? If we were able to ask this prophet of the late sixth century B.C.E. who he was talking about, it is very doubtful that he would say, "Why, I'm speaking of Jesus, the Messiah, the Christ." Other answers have been offered: the Servant is the whole nation of Israel, a special portion of Israel, Second Isaiah himself (as the eunuch suggested), Jeremiah, Jehoiachin (Judah's king who was a captive in Babylonia), Moses, a future messianic king like David, or some unknown prophetic/eschatological figure. Before the seeming impasse of multiple possibilities, how can Christians justify the claim that "Jesus is the answer"?

Perhaps the way to begin is to accept Paul Hanson's suggestion that we quit trying to answer the eunuch's question with a name, and that we begin traveling "the avenue of inquiry into the central themes of the Servant passages and their relation to the overall message of Second Isaiah" (Hanson, *Isaiah 40–66*, 41). In doing so, we may be able to affirm the New Testament writer's conviction that Jesus completely embodies these themes, and at the same time, we may find in the Servant passages "an invitation to reflect on the responsibility of all those who acknowledge God's sovereignty and recognize the dependence of all creation on God's order of justice" (Hanson, 41). Read in this manner, not only will these passages speak in a unique way to the identity and task of Jesus of Nazareth, but they also will provide a challenge for all the people of God to focus on their own relationship to God and on their mission before God.

> "Although dozens of candidates have been advanced as the person or group designated as the Servant, the matter is as confused as ever. . . . It seems in violation of the poetic tenor of the material to try to pin down the meaning of the Servant to one individual, one class, or, for that matter, one time."—Paul D. Hanson, *Isaiah 40–66*, Interpretation, 41.

Apart from the Servant Songs, a quick survey of the Old Testament will show that the title of YHWH's servant is not infrequently given, and those who receive it are certainly models of faith for us to emulate. They are as all believers should be. YHWH calls Abraham "my servant" in a speech to Isaac in Genesis 26:24. Within the context of prayers directed to YHWH, both Isaac and Jacob are referred to as servants (Gen. 24:14; 32:10). Exodus 14:31 calls Moses YHWH's servant (notice also the multiple uses of the title "servant of YHWH" as another name for Moses in Joshua), and YHWH confirms that opinion in Numbers 12:7. God also names Caleb "my servant" in Numbers 14:24. As kings of Israel, both Saul and David are called YHWH's anointed (messiah), but only David is acknowledged as YHWH's servant (2 Sam. 3:18; 7:5, 8). Elijah (2 Kings 9:36), Jonah (2 Kings 14:25), Isaiah (Isa. 20:3), and Job (Job 1:8) are YHWH's servants. YHWH may even speak of King Nebuchadrezzar of Babylon as "my servant" (Jer. 25:9; 27:6)! No wonder Second Isaiah understands that YHWH has declared "You are my servant" to Israel/Jacob (Isa. 41:9, see also v. 8) in the chapter prior to introducing the Servant Songs. It is both the ideal and a real possibility that every believer should become a servant of YHWH.

The First Servant Song

The first Servant passage, Isaiah 42:1–9, introduces the figure of YHWH's servant. In the first verse, God chooses, empowers, and commissions the servant. The choice of the servant is revealed to oth-

ers, "Here is my servant . . . my chosen." This presentation is remi-
niscent of YHWH's designation of Saul as king (1 Sam. 9:17 and 1
Sam. 10:24). Indeed, there is something
royal about the servant figure. Both
Psalms 18 and 89 celebrate God's choice
of David as king, and both psalms
acknowledge that David is the Lord's
servant. The king of Israel was the "servant of the covenant God . . . entrusted
with the upholding of the divine
decrees" (Eichrodt, *Theology of the Old
Testament,* vol. 1, 439). The parts of the
Old Testament that were put into writ-
ing after the exile experience, however, demonstrate a remarkable
capacity for giving royal attributes to humanity in general. The
Priestly account of creation recounts that at the creation of
humankind God said, "Let them have *dominion*" (author's emphasis). Psalm 8 adds the royal traits of "glory" and "honor" to that of
"dominion" in its description of the makeup of human beings: "You
have . . . crowned them with glory and honor. You have given them
dominion over the works of your hands" (Ps. 8:5–6). As James Luther
Mays has written, "The generic human being is an official in the
administrative arrangement of the kingdom of God. . . . On the
authority of the Genesis passages, the psalmist has put the entire race
in the status of a king" (Mays, *Psalms,* 66–67). The book of Job adds
to our understanding of humanity's royal status in the discourse
between Job and YHWH (Job 38–42). In his remarkable commentary on Job, Gerald Janzen indicates that Second Isaiah is similar to
Mark, Matthew, and Philippians: "In these portrayals, the central figure is set forth as suffering in the service of God, and as serving God
through suffering. . . . That suffering servant also is a royal figure"
(Janzen, *Job,* 258).

Furthermore, Janzen interprets the theme of "dust and ashes" in
terms closely related to Second Isaiah's presentation of the servant.
Job's confession to be dust and ashes (Job 42:6) is his acceptance of
the "vocation of humanity." This confession includes an awareness of
his creaturely existence and a royal concern for justice (*mishpat*),
which in the service of YHWH is redefined and allows itself to
become vulnerable to innocent suffering. Second Isaiah, then, presents the figure of the servant as one that potentially may find its fulfillment in any member of God's elect, the community of faith.

> **Who was the Servant?**
> Many answers have been given about the
> identity of the servant in these passages.
> According to the New Testament, Jesus is
> the servant. Others say, however, that the
> servant is the nation of Israel, Second Isaiah
> himself, Jeremiah, King Jehoiachin, Moses,
> or a future messianic king like David.

The commission of the servant is clearly stated in the first Servant Song: "He will bring forth justice to the nations . . . he will faithfully bring forth justice" (Isa. 42:1d, 3c). Paul Hanson offers an excellent discussion of justice, which in the Old Testament is understood as "the order of compassionate justice that God has created and upon which the wholeness of the universe depends" (Hanson, *Isaiah 40–66*, 42; note the entire discussion on pp. 42–44). Within our culture, we like to think of justice as an impartial force at work. We picture Lady Justice blindfolded, holding the scales of justice in her hands. Justice, we say, should not see skin color, economic position, educational status, or any other aspect of the contending parties that might prejudice the outcome of a case. Only the facts should count and "the truth, the whole truth, and nothing but the truth" should be the goal.

The Old Testament has a different model of justice. Since justice is part of God's order, it is not impartial and aloof. Perhaps the encounter between the prophet Nathan and King David best illuminates this understanding of justice (2 Sam. 12:1–6). Nathan tells the story of a rich man with many sheep who steals a poor man's single pet lamb to feed his guests rather than killing one of his own flock. David, the king who is in charge of justice in Israel, does not ask to hear both sides of the story. Instead, he jumps to the defense of the poor, helpless, and wronged man. Of course, for David, his zeal for justice took on a surprising meaning (2 Sam. 12:7–15). Nevertheless, it clearly shows the Old Testament idea of justice: God is on the side of the oppressed, and justice is established by means of personal, compassionate activity on behalf of those who are weak. The servant will bring justice to those who are usually ignored and left to die, the "bruised reeds" and "dimly burning wicks" of society (v. 3). The servant's justice will not depend upon strong-arm tactics and overwhelming force (v. 2). How the servant will bring about this justice will be made clearer in other Servant Songs, but this first song makes it clear that this justice is not limited to Israel. It is for "the nations" (vv. 1, 6) and "the earth" (v. 4) because YHWH, the God of justice, created the heavens and the earth and gave life to all people (v. 5). Indeed, "the coastlands wait" for the servant (v. 4)!

> "Everything for the servant, who has no self-possessed resources, depends on Yahweh. But Yahweh is faithful. As a consequence, this servant, who holds little promise of effectiveness, will not fail. The mission is as sure as is Yahweh's own fidelity—utterly sure!"—Walter Brueggemann, *Isaiah 40–66*, Westminster Bible Companion, 113.

68

The first Servant Song makes clear that the choice of the servant proceeds out of the mystery of God's election, "in whom my soul delights" (v. 1). The empowerment of the servant also comes only from God, "I have put my spirit upon him" (v. 1). Other Servant Songs will explain more of this empowerment; it is enough with the first song to simply state it. The idea of the suffering of the servant is only hinted at in the first song as well: "He will not grow faint or be crushed until he has established justice in the earth" (v. 4). More will be said of suffering later. What is important here, however, are not the details of that suffering, but the assurance that in spite of the possibility of suffering, there is no possibility of defeat.

The Second Servant Song

The second Servant Song (Isa. 49:1–13) amplifies certain aspects of the first song. The universal nature of the servant's commission presents itself in the very first words of the song as the servant addresses the coastland populations and the people of far away. The nature of this wider commission is the main subject of the poem. The song, however, also expands our insight into the choice of the servant (vv. 1, 5a) and our understanding of the servant's empowerment (v. 3).

YHWH's choice of the servant is no sudden decision. The one who is committed to God has the conviction that God's calling (choice) was present even before one's physical birth. YHWH forms the servant in the womb for this very purpose (v. 5a). That divine choice is communicated and sealed with a name while the servant is still in the mother's womb (v. 1). Such a conviction of God's call was certainly influenced by the prophet Jeremiah's understanding of his call (Jer. 1:5). Just as the servant is a royal figure, he is also a prophetic figure. Nevertheless, such a conviction is not limited to the prophets. Psalm 139:1–16 expresses a similar awareness of YHWH's total involvement in the life of any believer. This awareness includes all space, conditions, and time, even the time in the womb (v. 13) and includes a purpose for life itself (v. 16). The poet declares that for YHWH's servant, life is not accidental; it is purposeful from the very beginning.

The first Servant Song spoke only of the empowerment of the servant as a work of the Spirit of God: "I have put my spirit upon him" (Isa. 42:1c). Isaiah 49:2 describes poetically the equipping of the servant by the Spirit. The power given to the servant is neither political nor military. The servant's power is the word of his mouth. It will be a sword and an arrow. The Spirit-filled message of the servant will attack evil and penetrate deeply. The sword is sharp; the arrow is polished. The servant, as an instrument of the Spirit, will be effective in close personal encounters (sword) and confrontations at a distance (arrow).

If the phrases that describe the servant as a sharp sword and polished arrow are parallel and similar in meaning, then the other two phrases of the verse should also have a parallel significance: "in the shadow of his hand he hid me" and "in his quiver he hid me away." Some see these words as assurances of God's protective activity in the life of the servant. Surely the word "shadow/shade" may symbolize God's protection. The psalmist speaks of finding refuge "in the shadow of your [YHWH's] wings" (Ps. 57:1; 63:7), and declares, "The Lord is your shade at your right hand" (Ps. 121:5). Nevertheless, the phrase "the shadow of your [YHWH's] hand" is unique to Second Isaiah (49:2 and 51:16). While in Isaiah 51:16 "the shadow of his hand" may be a poetic way of expressing "the protection of his might," the parallelism in Isaiah 49:2 suggests that the significance of "shadow" may be something other than protection. After all, "shadow" also functions as a symbol of the brevity of human life (see Ps. 144:4).

In Isaiah 49:2, the meaning of "in the shadow of his hand he hid me" must be parallel in meaning to the phrase "in his quiver he hid me away." The second phrase is a metaphor in which the servant is an arrow. An arrow is not placed in a quiver so much to protect it as to keep it close at hand. Although it is out of sight, it is ready to use at an instant's notice. The first phrase is part of a simile in which the servant is like a sword, and raises two questions. How can a sword be hidden in someone's hand? What, exactly, is the "shadow of a hand"? We would expect a sheath to parallel a quiver. Perhaps the "shadow of a hand" refers to that spot on the thigh that is covered by a man's hand when he stands straight. That would be the location of the hilt of a sword in its sheath. Or perhaps God has something up the divine sleeve. Does this phrase refer to a concealed weapon? Could the sword be a switchblade? By this reading, the servant is a blade at hand, hidden but ready to use at an instant's notice. YHWH does not have to go back home to get a sword or round up some arrows. YHWH does not require time to prepare them for battle. The sword is already sharp, the arrow is already polished, and they lie close at hand. The servant is YHWH's minuteman, empowered by YHWH's Spirit for immediate action.

What immediate action is the servant's task? The task for which the servant has been commissioned seems to be twofold: He is to bring the covenant people back to YHWH (v. 5), and he is to be the means of accomplishing the salvation of all peoples of all nations (v. 6). The commission may be expressed, however, as one single task: He is to glorify YHWH (v. 3). In this song, the servant shares with the "peoples from far away" (v. 1) the story of his commission from YHWH. He reports that his effort in the first part of that commission, directed toward Jacob/Israel, was a failure. Though he tried with all his might, the results were negative. Everything, the servant thought, had been in vain (v. 4). Surprisingly, however, YHWH honors the servant (v. 5b) and broadens his commission to include the salvation of all the nations (v. 6)!

While the servant of YHWH would certainly have preferred to be heard and heeded in his ministry to God's people, he should have known, as Paul did, that "in the Lord your labor is not in vain" (1 Cor. 15:58). The servant may have been frustrated, but God's purposes had not failed. The servant's mission, like that of Isaiah of Jerusalem, seemed to be summed up in the commission: "Make the mind of this people dull, and stop their ears, and shut their eyes, so that they may not look with their eyes, and listen with their ears, and comprehend with their minds, and turn and be healed" (Isa. 6:10). But the servant's mission was larger than leading Israel to repentance. It was to glorify YHWH, and even failure in the first phase of the servant's mission could be used by YHWH in his determination to be glorified in the servant.

"The mission of the servant is quite different from that of the messiah promised by psalmists and other prophets. That conquering ruler would break the nations 'with a rod of iron' (Ps. 2:9), 'filling them with corpses' (Ps. 110:6). The servant, by contrast, is to proclaim liberation and to be a light to Israel [and] a light to the whole world."—William M. Ramsay, *The Westminster Guide to the Books of the Bible* (Louisville, Ky.: Westminster John Knox Press, 1994), 198.

If the servant could not accomplish even the "light" task of restoring the covenant people, how could he hope to share YHWH's salvation to the ends of the earth? The task would be accomplished only by means of the power of YHWH, a power that seems to be failure and defeat in the eyes of the world's kings and princes (v. 7). The Servant Songs of Second Isaiah seem to express a theology of the servant that embraces this apparent failure. Because the servant failed in the task of moving Israel/Jacob to repentance, the nation perished and the people suffered exile. Nevertheless, because the covenant people are spread around the globe in exile, it becomes possible for the nations to experience the salvation offered by YHWH, which is made

known through the servant's ministry to covenant community. Finally, the community's witness to YHWH's power to save will become that much more convincing when YHWH restores the covenant people back to Israel once again (vv. 8–12). These songs are forerunners of the theological position expressed by Paul in Romans 9–11. What was offered to Israel was then offered to the whole world; what is experienced by the world will also be experienced by Israel. That is why

Who was the suffering servant?

the servant can call on all of creation, heaven and earth and mountain, to praise YHWH for the comfort and compassion that is shown to YHWH's people, the "suffering ones," whether they are Jews or Gentiles (v. 13).

The Last Two Servant Songs

The final two Servant Songs (Isa. 50:4–9; 52:13–53:12) deepen our understanding of the significance of suffering in the ministry of the servant. The servant is to be a teacher (50:4). According to both songs, the teaching elicits rejection and suffering. But more importantly, the Spirit of God enables the servant, as Hanson writes, "to accept the hostility his message evokes with the quiet confidence that the final victory lies with those who are faithful to God" (Hanson, *Isaiah 40–66*, 140). The servant challenges YHWH's adversaries and encourages YHWH's people. The servant who is so despised, rejected, wounded, crushed, and bruised (53:3–5) in some way brings healing and strength to the people of God.

"Who will contend with me? Let us stand up together. Who are my adversaries? Let them confront me. It is the Lord GOD who helps me; who will declare me guilty?"— Isaiah 50:8–9.

If we are not to seek to identify the servant as a figure locked in history either as the nation of Israel or only in the person of Jesus

Christ, but are to find potential meaning in the figure of the servant that applies to every believer, what does this suffering mean? Is there a suffering that one can willingly embrace that will benefit the community of faith?

My years in Peru were during a time of poverty, suffering, and terrorism. Within this context, we worked in a church that sought to minister to a community struggling to form itself in the desert on the outskirts of the city of Trujillo. None of the members of the church had much money, but they did everything possible to minister to the physical as well as spiritual needs of the people in the community. The church began to help a family in which the father was disabled. His legs were run over by a bus while he was repairing an automobile. The church helped this family with food, hospital bills, and other expenses. The people offered the family friendship, prayer, and support through a long, painful ordeal. The family began attending church, and eventually the mother, father, and oldest daughter made professions of faith, accepting Jesus Christ as Lord.

I baptized them. Then the mother disappeared for about a month. When she returned, she stepped to the front of the congregation after the worship service in order to address her friends and neighbors. Her story was a complete surprise to me and to many others. Luisa confessed that she had been a member of Sendero Luminoso (Shining Path), a terrorist movement. She was a terrorist! She then told what had happened to her because of her Christian commitment. When the other members of the terrorist cell discovered that Luisa had become an evangelical Christian, they were afraid that she might confess and turn in the other members of the cell. So they kidnapped her and took her to Lima. For about a month, she had been punished and forced to participate in terrorist activity so that she could not turn anyone in without incriminating herself. She managed to escape and came back to Trujillo. That Sunday morning, she confessed her past to the church and ended her speech with these words: "I will never go back! I don't care if they kill me; I will never go back. I am a Christian now!" What Hanson wrote about the servant is embodied in Luisa: "The Servant did not submit to affliction through pathetic resignation but as a bold choice to participate with God in an act aimed at breaking the stranglehold that sin had maintained for countless ages over the human family" (Hanson, 159–60).

This poor, oppressed Peruvian woman who once saw armed revolution as a way toward a better life expressed a faith in Jesus Christ that made all the difference for her life and that of her family. She showed courage, love, and hope in spite of the many ways she had suffered. Luisa was never bothered by the terrorists again after her public declaration. She became a respected church leader who strengthened the fellowship so that others were healed by her bruises and made whole by her punishment (Isa. 53:5). Her commitment to the cause of Christ and her willingness to die for God's purpose in her life led me to a renewed commitment of my life and ministry to Jesus Christ. Luisa was a fulfillment of Isaiah 53:11: "The righteous one, my servant, shall make many righteous."

> "It is significant to observe that in Acts 8, when the eunuch asked about the identity of the Isaianic servant, Philip did not simply identify him with Jesus of Nazareth. Rather, beginning with the scriptures, 'he preached to him the good news of Jesus.' The suffering servant retains its theological significance within the Christian canon because it is inextricably linked in substance with the gospel of Jesus Christ, who is and always has been the ground of God's salvation of Israel and the world."—Brevard S. Childs, *Isaiah*, Old Testament Library, 424.

The Servant Songs develop an amazing picture of a person or a people who are completely committed to YHWH. It is a commitment that yields everything to the will of YHWH and depends on the Spirit of YHWH for direction, strength, and support. The way of YHWH is embraced even if that way involves suffering or death. The servant is so identified with YHWH and with others that the life of the servant, including suffering and death, functions to reconcile the two. Through a mystery of YHWH's Spirit, the servant is a person/people for others, both as a representative and as a vicarious substitute. The servant belongs to YHWH.

 Want to Know More?

About the Servant Songs?   See Werner H. Schmidt, *Old Testament Introduction*, 2d ed. (Louisville, Ky.: Westminster John Knox Press, 1995), 264–67.

About the theological concept of suffering?   See *The Westminster Dictionary of Christian Theology*, ed. Alan Richardson and John Bowden (Philadelphia: Westminster Press, 1983), 555–56.

Perhaps the identity of the servant will always be a matter of debate. There is an ambiguity in the portrait of the servant that is intentional. By faith, the Christian witness may well claim that Jesus of Nazareth is the Suffering Servant. In doing so, however, the church does not empty the figure of the servant of any other meaning. Instead, it is laying claim to the multiple layers of meaning found in the Servant Songs to better proclaim the significance of the life, suffering, death, and resurrection of the Lord Jesus Christ. Nevertheless within the faith communities of both Jew and Christian, The songs of the servant challenge the individual believer and the community as a whole to become such a servant.

❓ Questions for Reflection

1. Is Jesus the person described in the Suffering Servant passages? Paul Hanson and other scholars suggest that we stop trying to answer that question and focus instead on the central themes of these four passages. Is that an easy or difficult thing to do? Why is there such a temptation to identify Jesus as the servant (just as there was in unit 4 to identify the child, Immanuel, as the coming Messiah)?

2. Some of the most important figures in the Bible are referred to as servants of God, including Abraham, Isaac, Jacob, Moses, David, Jonah, Isaiah, and Job. What do these people have in common? What does their example say about what it means to be a servant?

3. What is the significance of the connection of the word "suffering" with the concept of servanthood? Can you be a true servant of God without suffering?

4. Identify some examples of suffering servants in modern-day history. What was it about those people that made them servants? In what ways did they suffer? (Remember that suffering is not just physical.)

8 Isaiah 44:9–20

YHWH and Idols

Every Sunday as I was growing up, we had roast beef for lunch. Before we went to church, Mother would put the roast, potatoes, and carrots in a Dutch oven, turn the oven on low, and we would leave the house. By the time we arrived home, a wonderful dinner was ready.

Every Monday as I was growing up, we had roast beef hash. I hate hash! "But we have to do something with the leftovers," Mother would remind me. Now that I am married, we also have roast beef for Sunday dinner at times. We, however, never have roast beef hash on Monday night . . . we have soup! "But we have to do something with the leftovers," I am reminded.

Leftovers may not get much respect around the dinner table, but Isaiah 44:9–20 tells of a case in which leftovers got too much respect from a woodsman who cut down a tree. "He burns half of it as a fire. Over this half, he eats meat, a roast he roasted, and he is satisfied. Furthermore, he warms himself and says, 'This is great! I'm comfortable. I've seen to the fire that I'll need.' And then he makes the leftovers into a god, his idol" (vv. 16–17a, au. trans.). The foolishness of a "leftover god" is at the heart of Second Isaiah's humorous satire about idols.

"There Is No Other Rock"

"All who make idols are nothing" (v. 9a) sets the tone for the entire passage. Some have called it a "taunt song." That may be a description of its form, but it does not describe the purpose of the passage in the book of Isaiah. Second Isaiah is not "in the face" of his Babylonian captor, ridiculing Babylonian religion. His purpose is to speak to the discouraged captives in order to keep the covenant people from idol worship! This is, as Paul Hanson has plainly stated, "a matter of life and death for a people threatened by assimilation into powerful pagan cults" (Hanson, *Isaiah 40–66*, 88). This passage is no reasoned exposition on the benefits of monotheism. Second Isaiah offers no explanation of the subtleties of the theology of an idol as a physical expression

> "If one theme can be identified as the cornerstone of the message of the eighth-century prophet Isaiah, it is the single-minded trust in God that banishes all false claimants to the human heart."—Hanson, *Isaiah 40–66*, 32.

of the presence of an invisible god. The prophet caricatures idol worship in such a way that any worshiper of YHWH would be forced to laugh at the foolishness of Babylonian worship and be ashamed to leave behind the worship of the true, living God to worship that which is false. In Isaiah 44:8, YHWH had declared, "Is there any god besides me? There is no other rock; I know not one." Then in 44:9, the prophet speaks of the futility of manufacturing and worshiping an "idol" (*pesel*), which in Hebrew originally referred to something hewed from a stone. YHWH, not an idol, is the true Rock.

The message does not stress, however, the claim that the *idol* is nothing. Here Second Isaiah claims that the ones who are involved in idol worship are nothing (*tohû*). One becomes like that which one worships. *Tohû* is a Hebrew word used to describe the desert as an empty wasteland (Deut. 32:10), or devastation that is a reversal of creation into chaos (Isa. 34:11). It is the absence of meaningful existence. Those who worship idols live futile, meaningless lives. The idols are incapable of doing anything that would profit (help) their makers. Because they do nothing, their worshipers experience nothing. The worshipers are called "witnesses" (v. 9), but they have seen nothing externally that their gods have done, nor have they internally "known" their gods in the sense of the intimacy of a personal relationship. As witnesses, therefore, they are put to shame; they have absolutely nothing to which they can testify in regard to the effective reality of their gods. They are shamed because they have foolishly wasted all of their efforts (v. 10) and because, as Knight translates a notoriously difficult verse 11, "their god turns out to be even less than human" (George A. F. Knight, *Deutero-Isaiah*, 116). A nothing god makes for a nothing people.

Second Isaiah then offers two descriptions of the manufacture of idols in order to make two statements about idol worship. The first, in a single verse, depicts the work of an ironsmith (v. 12). Using precise technical language, the prophet describes the hot, strenuous toil of a smith manufacturing a god. A human being wears himself out to make a physical object. Famished, parched, and fatigued, the smith winds up with an idol that can do nothing to meet his needs. He faints. What a contrast between this maker/worshiper of idols and the one who worships YHWH! "Those who wait for the Lord shall renew their strength, they shall mount up with wings like eagles, they shall run and not be weary, they shall walk and not faint" (Isa. 40:31).

> **What is an idol?**
> An idol is a statue or image of a god that is designed to be an object of worship.

Picking Up Gods

Isaiah 46 reveals the prophet making a similar point about the difference in the relationship that exists between worshiper and deity in the religion of Babylon and the religion of Israel. There the prophet describes a scene in which the images of the Babylonian gods Bel (i.e., Marduk) and Nebo (Marduk's son, the speaker for the gods) are loaded onto beasts of burden. It is probably a religious procession during the celebration of a religious festival that the prophet witnesses. Like floats at Mardi Gras, the heavy idols are moving down the streets lined with spectators. Then an animal stumbles or a cart hits a rut and the idols lurch from their perches. The attendant priests rush over and struggle to restore the idols to their places, but they cannot keep them from falling. "Bel bows down, Nebo stoops . . . they cannot save the burden" (Isa. 46:1–2). Men have to pick up their gods, and suddenly the scene is transformed for the prophet. It is no longer a religious procession he sees, but the certain defeat of Babylon. Then, too, men will be picking up their gods, loading them on beasts of burden to carry them to safety in the face of the approaching enemy. These gods are powerless to save their people, "but themselves go into captivity" (v. 2).

> "Those under the load of idolatry do not know the lift the living God can give."

Religion can become a burden. Idolatry transforms worship into a load rather than a lift. The ceremony of worship becomes an economic burden (Isa. 46:6), and the practice of religion exists as the constant, futile human struggle to guarantee stability and security through the manipulation of an idol. "They lift it to their shoulders, they carry it, they set it in its place, and it stands there; it cannot move from its place. If one cries out to it, it does not answer or save anyone from trouble" (Isa. 46:7). Those under the load of idolatry do not know the lift that the living God can give. YHWH addresses the covenant people as those "who have been borne by me from . . . birth, carried from the womb" (Isa. 46:3). YHWH promises, "Even to your old age I am he, even when you turn gray I will carry you. I have made, and I will bear; I will carry and will save" (Isa. 46:4). A personal relationship with the living God, not the routine of religious ritual, enables one to sing "Love Lifted Me."

Second Isaiah does not simply condemn the idolatry of Babylon, however, in this passage. By destroying any basis for idol worship, the prophet proclaims the uniqueness of YHWH and the exclusive claims of the worship of YHWH upon the life of the believer. This message of the prophet of the sixth century (B.C.E.) connects with the preaching of the eighth century (B.C.E.) Isaiah of Jerusalem. As Hanson writes, "If one theme can be identified as the cornerstone of the message of the eighth-century prophet Isaiah, it is the single-minded trust in God that banishes all false claimants to the human heart" (Hanson, 32). For Isaiah of Jerusalem, these "false claimants" consisted of both idols (Isa. 2:20–21) and the fraudulent worship of YHWH (Isa. 1:11–14), that is, a ritual of worship that does not include a lifestyle of justice and righteousness (Isa. 1:17). Israel's only hope lay in repentance and trust in YHWH alone. One day, Isaiah proclaimed, the people would turn and be able to say, "Surely God is my salvation; I will trust, and will not be afraid, for the LORD God is my strength and my might; he has become my salvation" (Isa. 12:2). That is why Second Isaiah could say, "Remember the former things of old; for I am God, and there is no other; I am God, and there is no one like me" (Isa. 46:9). Both prophets were convinced that salvation was to be found only through a personal relationship with YHWH that was complete, exclusive, and life changing. Any other practice of religion would be only a tremendous load borne by a staggering, helpless people.

> "It is important to remember that the Jews in exile were living as a minority in the shadows of the great Marduk temples. . . . Polemic that was waged against the claims of the Marduk priests therefore was not the idle activity of sophists. It was a matter of life and death for a people threatened by assimilation into powerful pagan cults."— Hanson, *Isaiah 40–66*, 88.

Empty Ritual?

Is it possible that even our own practice of Christianity could become a burden? Of course there are times when we all feel frantic and hassled in our attempts to worship. We can identify with the frustrated young woman who had a particularly bad morning one Sunday. While her husband showered, shaved, dressed, and read the paper, she was busy dressing herself, as well as dressing and feeding a five-year-old daughter and an infant son. She finally began herding the five-year-old out to the car when the infant spit up all over the mother's dress. It was too late to change, so she just wiped off what she could and decided to go to church smelling like sour milk, once again. Soon everyone was strapped in the car. As the car was backing out of the driveway, the five-year-old saw their neighbor dressed in shorts, lounging by his pool and reading the paper. "Mother," she whined, "why do we always have to go to church? The Smiths never go to church." The young woman whirled around to face her daughter and hissed through gritted teeth, "But don't you know, THEY'RE miserable!" If some do not understand that feeling, then perhaps they have not gone to church enough.

The threat of Christianity becoming a burden, however, is more profoundly portrayed in Leonard Bernstein's *Mass*. It is the burden of sustaining an empty, elaborate ritual rather than being sustained by the living God. The musical begins with the celebrant on stage alone, casually dressed in blue jeans. He accompanies himself on the guitar as he sings to God "a simple song." As the program continues, he is joined by more and more of the cast. The stage becomes crowded with artifacts of worship, and the celebrant is encumbered with increasingly elaborate robes. At the height of worship, weighted down with ceremonial vestments, he is barely able to lift the cup. The cast is dancing around him as the music becomes wilder and the words become bawdy. It is all too much for the celebrant. He smashes the chalice to the floor, spilling wine and breaking dreams. Everything has gone wrong and the burden is too much to bear. Only when the stage is littered and empty does the celebrant shed his robes, pick up the guitar, and once again establish a meaningful relationship with God through the singing of his own simple song of love, worship, and dedication.

The prophet has made his point in Isaiah 44:12: The burden of idolatry is that it drains rather than sustains. Any worship that focuses on anything other than a loyal, loving relationship with the living God is unsatisfying and empty. In verses 13–20, Second Isaiah makes another point: In the final analysis, the adoration of idols is self-serving and unworthy to be called worship. Once again, the text describes the tremendous effort that goes into making a god. This time, the effort is described in several verses instead of one, emphasizing the magnitude of that effort. The fact that the effort is expressed in a reversed order in verses 13–14 indicates the misguided nature of the endeavor. The carpenter decides, "Let us make god in man's image." The carving is

The burden of idolatry is that it drains rather than sustains.

described with precision and detail, from the snapping of the first chalk line to the final shaving stroke of the carpenter's plane. The cutting of the tree, a choice cedar, holm, or oak is detailed. Perhaps the carpenter has gone to great expense and great distances to obtain the tree, because the cedar is not native to Babylon. The tree is allowed to grow to stately, majestic proportions. There may even be an attempt to plant and cultivate the non-native trees there in Babylon (v. 14). It takes a long time to make a god!

A Leftover God

The following verses, however, are most revealing. In them, the prophet describes the activity of the carpenter three times, and each retelling becomes more elaborate. Verse 15 shows the use made of this important, expensive, majestic timber. The idol maker first uses it as fuel to meet personal needs: warmth and food. In spite of the meticulous description of the idol maker's efforts in verses 13–14, those efforts are, in reality, only secondary. The human needs preempt those of the god. The prophet assures the reader that such a reading of verse 15 is no mistake because it is repeated in verses 16–17, complete with the carpenter's own words. First, he compliments himself,

"This is great! I am comfortable. I've seen to the fire that I'll need." Then, after he has secured his own needs, he says to the idol, "Save me, for you are my god!" (v. 17). All that work for the gods was actually self-serving. The idol maker's desires came first. The carpenter fashions the god from the leftovers. A leftover god never has first place in the life of the devotee. A leftover god is never worthy of first place.

> "I am the LORD your God . . . ; you shall have no other gods before me. You shall not make for yourself an idol. . . . You shall not bow down to them or worship them; for I the LORD your God am a jealous God. . . ."
> —Exodus 20:2–5

The prophet describes the carpenter's activity a third time. This time, however, the carpenter is not alone; the whole of the idolatrous people is included in the "they" of v. 18. Once again, the first activity is self-preservation: burning, baking, roasting, and eating. The leftovers are used for an object of worship.

The prophet puts condemning words in the people's mouth. They do not speak of a god or even an idol. They confess to making an abomination and falling down before nothing but a block of wood in activity that falls far short of worship (v. 19). The idol worshiper has truly become like the idol that is worshiped. The idol cannot save (v. 17), and the idol worshiper "cannot save himself" (v. 20). The whole enterprise of idol worship is revealed to be a feeding on ashes in which the worshipers are so deluded that they are unable to look objectively at themselves and ask, "Is not this thing in my right hand a fraud?" (v. 20).

> "In order to appreciate this text as a resource for faith, it is necessary to contrast Yahweh to the would-be gods of our time and place. In the United States, the rival gods are likely the icons of free market capitalism that run from entertainment celebrities and sports heroes to the 'bull market' to the generative power of television ads, all of which seek to seduce us into a cozy world of private safety and happiness. From the perspective of this text, these 'idols' are fake precisely because they have no power to keep their promises."—Walter Brueggemann, *Isaiah 40–66*, Westminster Bible Companion, 69.

The contrast drawn by the prophet is that of a god which is satisfied with leftovers and the living God who will not accept them. Self-serving activity in worship is always idolatrous. Whether it is a god fashioned from leftovers or an attempt to worship the Lord through the offering of the leftovers of life, the real god being adored is self. As surely as God cannot be made from scrap, neither will God accept whatever scraps we are willing to give. Believing that God would is a fraudulent delusion that blinds the worshipers (v. 18) and leaves them without any spiritual nourishment (v. 20).

At a community Thanksgiving worship service, the minister had the responsibility to present the children's sermon. He called all the children to the front of the sanctuary. As they were seated around him, he started pulling items from two grocery sacks. "One for me, two for me, three for me, . . . sixteen for me, seventeen for me, . . . twenty-nine for me, and thirty for me!" Of course the children objected, saying that he was being selfish. The consensus was that since he was in church, he should at least share with God.

The minister agreed with the children and shared a verse or two about the tithe and explained that tithing means to give one tenth of our possessions to God. He then began recounting and separating the groceries. "One for me, two for me, three for me, . . . eight for me, nine for me, and one for God." Then he asked the children if they were satisfied with this new arrangement. It seemed fair to them and they were happy. The minister, however, said that God was still not satisfied. The gifts had been presented in the wrong order. God does not want to receive what is last, rather God deserves the first and the best. In a very powerful moment, he again recounted everything, "One for God, one for me, two for me, three for me . . ." The greatness and generosity of God were etched anew in the minds of children and adults. The true and living God cannot be worshiped with leftovers.

God and leftovers are mutually exclusive. Any form of worship that seeks to serve God with the leftovers of life is idolatry. Second Isaiah's scathing satire of Babylonian religion condemns more than the manufacture of idols. It makes it clear that at the very heart of idolatry is selfishness; all the perceived needs of the worshiper have priority over the service of the god. The prophet declares that any god that is adequately

 Want to Know More?

About idols? See Donald K. McKim, *The Westminster Dictionary of Theological Terms* (Louisville, Ky.: Westminster John Knox Press, 1996), 137; *The Westminster Dictionary of Christian Theology*, Alan Richardson and John Bowden, eds., 280–81.

served with leftovers is incapable of acting to save the worshiper or itself. Those who worship a leftover god have deluded themselves. Ultimately they wear themselves out for nothing. They have nothing for a god, they receive nothing from their god, and their worship, to which they contribute nothing but leftovers, means nothing. "All who make idols are nothing" (Isa. 44:9).

? Questions for Reflection

1. What idols does our society create and worship? What idols do *you* create and worship? Is it difficult in our consumeristic society to keep from worshiping idols? Why?

2. As a group, list other scripture passages in which the worship of idols is condemned. What is the overriding message of all of these passages? Or is there more than one message?

3. Read again and discuss the comments about the possibility of Christian practice becoming a burden. Have you ever felt like the frantic young woman mentioned in this unit? Like the five-year-old with all her questions? Like the neighbors in their pool?

4. One of the messages in this unit is that God is not satisfied with, and will not accept, our "leftovers." Give some examples of what you think is meant by "leftovers."

YHWH and the Word, Part Two

One of the amazing changes of the past twenty-five years has been the transformation of the average American from a producer to a consumer. The greatest contribution of average American citizens to the national economy is no longer measured by what they produce, but by what they buy. One major credit card company produces advertising campaigns that feature the excitement of a worldwide event, then warns not to take a competitor's credit card because it will not be honored. Its card is the only one that guarantees acceptance. Another major credit card company produces commercials that state the prices of various items, such as green fees, golf clubs, and golf balls, then lists an experience that cannot be bought, such as "a hole in one with a witness." The commercial concludes that some things are priceless, but for everything else this credit card will do. We want our credit to be good. We like to think that we can buy just about anything that we should ever need. For consumers, money is indeed the answer. That is why the message of Second Isaiah shocks our generation.

"Ho, everyone who thirsts, come to the waters; and you that have no money, come, buy and eat! Come, buy wine and milk without money and without price. Why do you spend your money for that which is not bread, and your labor for that which does not satisfy?" (Isa. 55:1–2a). These words do more than shock. They sting because we know deep down that simply consuming does not satisfy. We buy and buy and buy, but we never have enough. With our credit cards, we can obtain everything that has a price tag, but we know that those things without a price tag are what make the difference in life. Instinctively, we know that YHWH's water, wine, milk, and bread in this offer are not among those products that can be found on any grocery shelf. YHWH is not using these words to make consumers out of us. YHWH's word calls us into a new relationship as servants.

All Are Invited

Chapter 54 of Isaiah ended with an unusual phrase, "the heritage of the servants of the Lord. . . ." The concept of "the servant of YHWH" has become familiar to the reader of Second Isaiah, but this verse marks the first use of the plural form of YHWH's servant(s). Chapter 56 also uses the plural form in verse 6, which announces that even foreigners may "join themselves to the LORD, to minister to him, to love the name of the LORD, and to be his servants." According to the prophet, then, not all the "servants of YHWH" are Israelites, and evidently, not all Israelites are "servants of YHWH"! Only YHWH's servants will have a rich heritage and enjoy YHWH's vindication. Therefore, chapter 55 opens with an invitation to choose to be one of YHWH's servants. As Hanson rightly points out, "The everlasting covenant was now to be expanded beyond the privileged elite to embrace the entire community of those obedient to God's word" (Hanson, 179). That is why he can make the connection between this passage and the parable of the wedding feast in Matthew 22 (Hanson, 177). Everyone is invited, and only those who refuse to accept the invitation will be left out.

The urgency of the invitation is seen in the repeated imperatives of 55:1: "Come! . . . Come, buy and eat! . . . Come, buy!" YHWH assumes the role of a street vendor hawking his wares. The people are thirsty and hungry. They have choices, for there are other merchants in the street. The difficulty the people face is choosing the right vendor. Ignorance or foolishness can cost them dearly and leave them unsatisfied (v. 2). They must listen carefully to determine which vendor is truly best for them.

It is important to distinguish between different vendors. I will never forget a visitor that we had while we were missionaries in Peru. He had been in the country only a few days, but he had already seen several vendors in Lima and in downtown Trujillo, the city in which we lived. He had noticed that each vendor used a different call, whistle, pipe, or horn depending upon what product was for sale: ice cream, milk, candies, tamales, and so forth. Then one morning he heard the insistent clanging of a bell out on the street and called out to everyone in the house, "I don't know what it is, but we'd better get it while it's hot!" Rushing to the door, he discovered that this "vendor" was the garbage truck! "Why do you spend your money for that which is not bread, and your labor for that which does not satisfy?"

YHWH alone offers that which satisfies: salvation. It is symbolized in the first two verses by water, bread, wine, milk, and "rich food" (literally, *fatness*). Water and bread are the very basics for the sustenance of life. Wine, milk, and fatty meats are luxuries. The salvation that YHWH offers is life in all its abundance, both spiritual and physical. Certainly the water, wine, milk, bread, and fat are metaphors for the full blessings of the life of faith.

What street vendors do you choose?

Proverbs 9 has Lady Wisdom use these same elements in her invitation to her table (vv. 1–3), and verse 10 reveals this to be symbolic language teaching that "the fear of the LORD is the beginning of wisdom, and the knowledge of the Holy One is insight." Psalm 42:2 and the beatitude of Matthew 5:6 demonstrate that in both the Old and New Testaments, hunger and thirst, bread and water are symbols of the spiritual life. Nevertheless, we should not spiritualize these elements too much. For the prophet, the salvation of YHWH includes both a liberation from sin and a liberation from Babylon. The blessings of YHWH's covenant include both a joyous spiritual relationship with God and a fullness of physical life that includes a return to the land of Israel.

The Everlasting Covenant

The nature of the covenant is at issue in verses 3–5. Hanson has rightly pointed to Psalm 89 as a key to understanding the crisis of faith during the Babylonian exile (Hanson, 178). For the captives from Jerusalem, the covenant had found its chief expression through YHWH's promise to David (Ps. 89:3–4; see 2 Sam. 7:11–16). The destruction of Jerusalem, its temple, and the end of Judah's monarchy presented a tremendous challenge to such a theology. The only response seemed to be a sense of rejection (Ps. 89:39), doubt (Ps. 89:49), and a desperate plea (Ps. 89:50). Second Isaiah now offers another response to YHWH's promise from within the reality of exile: a reinterpretation of the covenant with David so that it now applies to every believer. David, indeed, had been YHWH's servant (Ps. 89:20), but now all are invited to be servants of YHWH. The "everlasting covenant" and YHWH's "steadfast, sure love for David" had not been negated. On the contrary, they were being expanded! All are invited to fulfill the role of David in the covenant as a witness (v. 4a), guide (leader, v. 4b), and "evangelist" (v. 5 declares "you shall call nations that you do not know").

> "In the name of the same God who invited *all* to the banquet, Second Isaiah announced that God's plan had not been defeated by the ruin of the royal house of David but rather that the everlasting covenant was now to be expanded beyond the privileged elite to embrace the entire community of those obedient to God's word."—Hanson, *Isaiah 40–66*, 179.

The imperatives of an urgent invitation found in verses 1–3 continue in verse 6: "Seek the LORD while he may be found, call upon him while he is near." To "seek YHWH" originally meant to participate in worship at a holy place, especially the temple (Ps. 24:3–6; 27:8; 63:1–2; see Deut. 12:5). Nevertheless, Second Isaiah stands closer to prophets such as Jeremiah (29:13) and Amos (5:4, 6) who understand "seeking YHWH" as a sincere repentance and reliance upon YHWH separate from any connection with religious ritual. It is, as Brueggemann suggests, "to draw near to Yahweh, to come to terms with Yahweh, to respond to Yahweh's offer" (Brueggemann, *Isaiah 40–66*, 160). The prophet offers a gracious invitation to a caring, personal relationship with YHWH. There is an urgency sounded in the invitation: "while he may be found . . . while he is near" (v. 6). Timing seems to be important. If there are times when YHWH may be found, are there times when YHWH may *not* be found? If there are times when God is near, are there times when God is *not* close by, or when divine help is unavailable?

What does the prophet have in mind when he uses the word "while"? Does he have in mind a "limited time only" offer from YHWH? Is Second Isaiah saying that there are only certain moments in history when God is willing to save, or that YHWH's salvation is limited to some chronological season? Certainly the prophet perceived the tremendous importance of his moment in history. YHWH was about to act in world events to bring about the liberation of captive Israel. It was an important time, a significant day (Isa. 49:8). The significance and urgency, however, cannot be traced to the date on the calendar; the importance of this day for the people of YHWH is that it is their present. The prophet's sense of urgency originates in an awareness of what theologian and philosopher Paul Tillich called the "eternal now," God's eternity breaking into the believer's present. Second Isaiah's urgent invitation declares that God's grace is available. The apostle Paul understood precisely the prophet's invitation and alludes to it in 2 Corinthians 6:2, "See, now is the acceptable time; see, now is the day of salvation!" The urgency of "seeking YHWH" now is not that YHWH will not be around later. "It is urgent," the prophet says to his people, "because this is your time." When will YHWH be found? "When you search for me, you will find me; if you seek me with all your heart" (Jer. 29:13). Such seeking is at the heart of Second Isaiah's timely invitation.

"They Have Chosen Death"

The invitation is followed in verse 7 by a summons to the life of faith that exhibits a sustained tension between grace and obedience. The prophet calls on the people to "return" (repent) for YHWH desires to display mercy and there is the assurance that YHWH "will abundantly pardon." This salvation is entirely a gift from YHWH. YHWH is the one who invites; the water, bread, meat, milk, and wine may be had without price; YHWH freely forgives because YHWH is merciful. The everlasting covenant YHWH offers in verse 3 is the embodiment of grace itself. The people can "seek the LORD" because God is already seeking them. They can call upon YHWH because YHWH has first called them. However, the people also have a responsibility: "Let the wicked forsake their way, and the unrighteous their thoughts" (v. 7). The people in exile, as Hanson notes, are in a situation whose origin "traces not to weakness or inattention on God's part. . . . Instead they have chosen death" (Hanson, 180). The death of their nation, the death of their way of life, the death of their faith are the consequences of their own actions. Therefore, they must abandon those choices ("ways" and "thoughts"). They must open their minds to God's thoughts and commit their lives to God's ways. A genuine willingness to turn one's life around, to express a trust in

YHWH through obedience, is the type of faith that is able to receive God's grace.

It is difficult to admit that one is wrong. The terms that Second Isaiah uses, translated as "wicked" and "unrighteous," are general terms for wrongdoers, but they leave no doubt about the people's guilt. "Wicked" means guilty of sin or guilty of a crime, and the phrase translated "unrighteous" (*'ish 'awen*) refers to the person who is an evildoer, one whose thoughts and actions produce trouble and sorrow. The use of such generalized terms is intentional on the part of the prophet for they may be applied to any self-serving attitude or activity. In fact, Hosea employed the term *'awen* to mean "idolatry" when he renames Bethel (House of God) "Beth-aven" (House of Idolatry/Evil/Guilt) in Hosea 4:15; 5:8; and 10:5 and when he condemns the "high places of idolatry" in 10:8. The very essence of idolatry is placing the self on the heart's throne, which belongs rightly to God. It is following the self's plan rather than God's, striking out on the self's road rather than taking God's path. Not only would refusing YHWH's invitation to return to the right roadway be a tragedy, but it would constitute the idolatrous sin of placing the self before God. The prophet calls on the people in exile to admit that they are indeed guilty and abandon all plans, attitudes, and activity that would keep them from being YHWH's obedient servants.

The tragedy of refusing to "return to the LORD" is a double tragedy. First of all, it fails to perceive the loving heart of God, who with mercy and grace makes pardon freely available to all who confess their need for mercy and grace and their complete inability to obtain it by any means of their own. What is more, their refusal to leave behind their thoughts and ways is to miss the opportunity to share in YHWH's thoughts and ways. It is like making one's own way to Lizard Lick and missing the free trip to Maui! "For as the heavens are higher than the earth, so are my ways higher than your ways and my thoughts than your thoughts" (v. 9). In drawing attention to the vast distinction between God's ways and thoughts and human ways and thoughts (vv. 8–9), the prophet is not simply saying that human logic cannot comprehend the plans of God. These words communicate the desire of YHWH to share such high, wonderful, and mysterious plans with all who would join the community of faith. A divine fellowship is formed in which God's servants can fully participate in God's plans. The invitation has been given. The options are clear. Why settle for anything less?

"I Am Reliable"

There is no need to settle for anything less. God's servants do not need to fear that God is offering more than can be delivered. This offer is the word of YHWH and the word of YHWH will never be an empty thing (v. 11, the Hebrew *dabar* means "word," "thing," "event"). The assurance that what YHWH says is not meaningless comes not from the prophet, but directly from YHWH. YHWH is the giver of many gifts, including snow and rain. There is nothing that humans may do to control these elements (still today we cannot even predict them with great accuracy!). Life, however, would be impossible without them. These elements water the earth and start a chain of events that sustains life. Human beings have a responsible role in that chain (v. 10b), but they neither initiate it nor control it. YHWH freely gives these things to creation and they effectively provide proof of YHWH's care. The effectiveness of YHWH's word is comparable to the effectiveness of these other works of YHWH. "I am reliable," declares YHWH.

This passage has more to say about the word of YHWH than simply that YHWH stands behind it. The word itself is an event (*dabar*) that is powerful and effective. The word is a part of YHWH's activity within history; it is a part of God's plan for creation. The word of YHWH has declared that Cyrus is the anointed of YHWH, whose purpose is to liberate Israel (45:1). It has called Israel to be a servant among the nations (49:3, 6). It has called prophet and citizens to be servants who look with confidence to YHWH for vindication and the confirmation of their heritage (54:17). The word of YHWH has set into motion the liberation of Israel. Even though Israel's salvation lies in the future, the word calls the people of faith to live as YHWH's free servants while still living under a Babylonian administration. The word of YHWH guarantees liberation. The word of YHWH effects that liberation wherever people of faith trust in it. As Hanson writes, "The Servant and the Word play closely related roles in relation to God's will in Second Isaiah" (Hanson, 182). The Word, like the Suffering Servant, brings YHWH's purposes to completion. For Second

> "It seems right to me that in so many instances in both the Hebrew scriptures and the gospels salvation is described in physical terms, in terms of the here and now, because I believe that this is how most of us first experience it. Only later do the more spiritual implications of salvation begin to make themselves known."—Kathleen Norris, *Amazing Grace: A Vocabulary of Faith* (New York: Riverhead Books, 1998), 20.

Isaiah, the realization of both lies beyond the time of his ministry. For the Christian community, their ultimate realization is found in Jesus Christ, who is the Word made flesh (John 1:14) and the Suffering Servant (Acts 8:30–35). Within the context of the whole book of Isaiah, the word of YHWH finds confirmation in Israel's return to Jerusalem from exile. That event is the primary referent of this word of YHWH.

"Led Back in Peace"

"For you shall go out in joy, and be led back in peace" (Isa. 55:12). The movement of the covenant people from Babylon to Jerusalem is a new exodus. As Brueggemann writes, "The term 'go out' . . . is an Exodus term" (Brueggemann, *Isaiah 40–66*, 162). Just as the Hebrew people moved from captivity to freedom in their journey from Egypt to Canaan, so those in exile would begin a journey toward freedom. This journey, however, would be characterized by joy. The first exodus was carried out in haste: The Hebrew people hurriedly ate a Passover meal while standing with their shoes on and while dressed in clothing made ready to move in flight (Ex. 12:11). This new exodus would be more like a parade of exuberant triumph. Second Isaiah began his message with a declaration that the people will come in a victory procession with YHWH at the head (Isa. 40:10) and in the light of day before all the peoples of the earth (Isa. 40:5). He closes his message repeating that declaration. The phrase promising that the people will "be led back in peace" is an example of the "divine passive"; YHWH is understood to be the one doing the leading. YHWH's leadership is always one of peace (*shalom*), a wholeness and well-being that provides everything that is needed. (Psalm 23 is an expression of trust in that leadership.)

> "This is the new Exodus undertaken, not in fear or in haste as the first Exodus, but in joy and peace, in well-being and calmness. The poetry . . . anticipates that there will be a triumphant parade of Jews headed home, with Yahweh at the head in exuberant well-being."—Walter Brueggemann, *Isaiah 40–66*, Westminster Bible Companion, 162.

Not only will this event be a new exodus, but it also will be, in some sense, a "new creation" (Hanson, 183). Creation is effected by the actions of God's people. The eighth century (B.C.E.) prophet Isaiah had seen a connection between Israel and nature in the working out of God's judgment. Creation had been a witness to YHWH's lawsuit against the covenant people (Isa. 1:2). The people's refusal to trust in YHWH would result in vineyards being transformed into briars and thorns (Isa. 7:23–25). Another eighth century prophet proclaimed that the people's idolatry in their search for fertility would result in futility in worship. "Thorn and thistle shall grow up on their altars" (Hos. 10:8). These prophets were drawing on ancient traditions within Israel's creation story: "Cursed is the ground because of you; in toil you shall eat of it all the days of your life; thorns and thistles it shall bring forth for you" (Gen. 3:17–18). In his message of YHWH's gift of salvation, Second Isaiah envisions a great reversal not only for Israel, but also for creation! "Instead of the thorn shall come up the cypress; instead of the brier shall come up the myrtle" (Isa. 55:13). The joy is not Israel's alone. Mountains and hills themselves will break forth into singing, and the trees will applaud at the procession moving toward freedom (55:12). Salvation does affect creation: "For the creation waits with eager longing for the revealing of the children of God; for the creation was subjected to futility, not of its own will but by the will of the one who subjected it, in hope that the creation itself will be set free from its bondage to decay and will obtain the freedom of the glory of the children of God" (Rom. 8:19–21). The biblical vision of salvation includes not only the seeing of the new Jerusalem (Rev. 21:2), but also the seeing of a new heaven and a new earth (Rev. 21:1).

Second Isaiah does not conclude, however, with an emphasis on either Israel or creation. Instead, his focus is entirely upon the one who is Lord of Israel and creator of the world, YHWH. This redemptive word/event of YHWH will be a memorial and sign that gives

 Want to Know More?

About salvation? See *The Westminster Dictionary of Christian Theology*, ed. Alan Richardson and John Bowden, 519–21.

witness to the effective power, dependable faithfulness, and loving grace that YHWH shows to all creation within the relationship between YHWH and the covenant people. According to the word of YHWH, salvation is freely offered to all who will accept it. There is nothing that can be substituted for God's high way of salvation, and this salvation will bring change, freedom, joy, and peace to all of God's creation. It is a word that shall never be nullified.

? Questions for Reflection

1. Read Matthew 22:1–4 and compare it to Isaiah 55:1. What do these two passages say about the kingdom of God? Are there other similar passages in scripture that come to mind?
2. Verse 7 talks about returning to God. Do you know people who have "returned to God"? Where had they been? Why had they gone away? Why had they come back? How were they received by the church? How do you think they were received by God?
3. Read 55:12 again. Why were these words so important to God's people to hear at the time they were written? What was the historical context?
4. According to the last few verses of Isaiah 55, the Lord will create a covenant relationship with God's people that "shall not be cut off." Talk about a time when you felt "cut off" from God. How did it feel? How long did it last? How did you reconnect with God?

YHWH and All Flesh

Mayfield County, Kentucky, was the scene of a church conflict in the late 1800s. The local Baptist church had two deacons who hated each other and opposed each other on any and every issue. One week, one of the deacons installed a small wooden peg in the wall at the back of the church for the minister to hang his hat on. When the other deacon found out about the peg, he became extremely angry because he had not been consulted in the matter. The congregation then took sides in the dispute, and eventually the church split. Through the 1980s, one could still travel to Mayfield County, Kentucky, and find the Anti-peg Baptist Church!

Now, I am a third-generation Baptist minister, so I can well believe this story. I recall my father often saying, "Wherever you can find two Baptists, you will find three different opinions." Nevertheless, we all know that Baptists have no monopoly on religious conflict. The contemporary Christian landscape continues to be marked by divisions that arise out of personal disputes (for example, the color of a carpet), doctrinal issues (for example, the ordination of women), or ethical debates (for example, abortion). Some of these divisions are as silly as a hat rack for the preacher, while others are obviously far more serious and complicated schisms. The people of God have always experienced conflicts and splits because they are, after all, people. What is true of Christian history is also true of Jewish experience. Isaiah 66 gives us a glimpse into the serious fractures within the covenant community

> "The prophetic pronouncement in chapter 66 . . . is a hard-hitting attack on those who would jeopardize Israel's future by substituting their human agendas for God's plan of universal salvation."—Paul D. Hanson, *Isaiah 40–66*, Interpretation, 248.

95

some years after its return to Jerusalem from the Babylonian exile.
The last chapter of the book of Isaiah seems to reflect three different, but related, conflicts. There is a single external issue of contention: the building of the temple. A second level of conflict, seen
from the perspective of the opponents to the temple, addresses the
nature of the true worship of YHWH. Finally, through these conflicts
a greater theological issue comes into view: the controversy of the
makeup of the true people of YHWH. This great, fundamental issue
lies at the base of the division within the worshiping community and
at the base of the disagreement over the need for a new temple.

Return from Exile

By 520 B.C.E., the people who had returned from the Babylonian exile
had been in Jerusalem for some eighteen years. They had come with
high expectations of all that YHWH would do for Jerusalem. Even
the words of Second Isaiah had seemed to promise honor, riches, and
political power upon Israel's restoration to Jerusalem (Isa. 49:22–23;
54:11–12). Instead of the prosperity that they had expected, the
returnees were living within a greatly reduced state under a governor
rather than a king. They suffered scarcities of food and drink, and
they endured a poverty generated by inflation (Hag. 1:5–11). After
nearly two decades of waiting, the crisis of faith demanded an answer.

The prophet Haggai proclaimed that the answer lay in building a
house/temple for YHWH. His preaching promised that the completion of the Temple would usher in an age of wealth, honor, and splen-
dor that had never before been known. While Haggai's message can
be readily understood as a prophetic critique of a society that places
its own desires above its devotion to YHWH, there was evidently a
group within the community that applied Haggai's oracles quite literally. "The Temple will guarantee prosperity," they taught. "Build
the Temple and YHWH will have to act. YHWH will finally put
Israel at the top of all the nations!"

Isaiah 66 records a prophetic voice raised in opposition to such an
understanding of "temple." Paul Hanson captures Third Isaiah's message clearly when he writes, "Every effort to establish the blessed reign
through human construction was doomed to failure, for it would
come up against the God who could not be deceived by human idols
and manipulative shrines" (Hanson, *Isaiah 40–66*, 248). With that
message, Third Isaiah placed himself squarely within a long biblical

tradition that opposes the belief that God's saving activity is guaranteed by the very existence of a temple, or that God's saving activity is limited by the absence of a temple.

The temple never offered to Israel any advantage or control over YHWH, according to this tradition. Israel, in its songs of worship, simultaneously recognized that YHWH "is in his holy temple" and that the throne of YHWH "is in heaven" (Ps. 11:4). Indeed, the heavenly throne of YHWH distinguishes Israel's God from all other gods who are but idols bound within the confines of their shrines (Ps. 113:4–5). YHWH knows no such limits. Even the royal temple tradition expresses the awareness of YHWH's transcendence through Solomon's prayer at the dedication of the temple: "Will God indeed dwell on the earth? Even heaven and the highest heaven cannot contain you, much less this house that I have built!" (1 Kings 8:27). The prophet Jeremiah specifically rejected the idea of any advantage given over YHWH by the presence of the temple in Jerusalem! His temple sermon warned, "Do not trust in these deceptive words: 'This is the temple of the LORD, the temple of the LORD, the temple of the LORD'" (Jer. 7:4; also see Jeremiah 26). Isaiah 66:1 is an expression of the same theme.

Read in this way, Third Isaiah is not necessarily against the temple as such, but he speaks against a trust in the temple that is distinct from a trust in YHWH. As a whole, the Isaiah tradition has a high regard for the temple itself. Isaiah 6 locates the commission of Isaiah of Jerusalem within the temple. The Isaiah tradition preserved in 2 Kings 19 records Isaiah's oracle giving YHWH's positive response to the prayer for deliverance that Hezekiah prayed in the temple when threatened by Sennacherib.

The prophet Haggai believed that a national crisis in faith could be cured by building a temple to YHWH.

Second Isaiah had included the establishment of the temple as part of YHWH's purpose in anointing Cyrus (Isa. 44:28). There is the recognition of YHWH speaking from

97

the temple by Third Isaiah himself (Isa. 66:6)! Isaiah 66:1, therefore, is a condemnation of a particular theology of the temple, a triumphal theology of success and prosperity based on something external and material rather than faith in YHWH alone. Third Isaiah represents a group that opposed the efforts of another religious element that was engaged in building the temple for the wrong reason. A temple established upon a false theology could only result in a false worship.

True Worship

True worship is the focus of a deeper level of conflict in Isaiah 66. For the prophet, the attitude of a person is more indicative of true worship than any specific activity. The NRSV understands Isaiah 66:3 as the equating of legitimate acts of temple worship with activities that are expressly forbidden by YHWH. The Hebrew text, which does not contain the comparative words "is like . . . like . . . like . . . like," may, however, be interpreted as accusing some of both worshiping in YHWH's temple and participating in pagan worship. Isaiah 66:3 would then be translated, "The one who slaughters an ox also practices human sacrifice . . . and the one who makes a memorial offering of frankincense also blesses idols." Such a reading is possible when read in light of Isaiah 66:17. While such syncretism would be a more serious charge, no matter which translation one chooses, the reason for Third Isaiah's condemnation of these acts of worship is that the worshipers themselves are not in right relationship with YHWH. They go their own way (Isa. 66:3). YHWH speaks, but they do not listen. They choose to do what is evil in YHWH's sight rather than that which would be pleasing to God (Isa. 66:4). Sacrifice, thank offerings, and memorial offerings mean nothing if they do not express a personal response of humility and reverence before YHWH (Isa. 66:2).

Once again, Third Isaiah stands within a biblical tradition that determines true worship by the attitude of the worshiper rather than the performance of specific acts. The book of Isaiah has already portrayed YHWH as one who condemns those that "draw near with their mouths and honor me with their lips, while their hearts are far from me" (Isa. 29:13). Other prophets such as Amos, Hosea, Micah, and Jeremiah do the same. Even within the songs sung during the worship at the temple there is an acknowledgment that sacrifices in no way enrich God or in some way meet YHWH's basic needs (Ps.

50:9–13). It profits the wicked nothing to recite God's statutes or to speak about the covenant (Ps. 50:16). The ones who do know God's benefits are those who live in gratitude for God's grace and demonstrate their relationship with God through right living (Ps. 50:23).

Evidently, Third Isaiah and his prophetic group made their opposition to the temple known as well as their critique of mere religious ritual. As a result, an opposing group then ridiculed them. They had already had their chance; if YHWH was going to act without a temple, there had already been ample opportunity during the past eighteen years! Where was the proof of Third Isaiah's preaching? "Let the LORD be glorified so that we may see your joy," his enemies demanded (Isa. 66:5). The opposition is real. As Brueggemann writes: "There is no easy way for serious faith" (Brueggemann, *Isaiah 40–66*, 254).

In the face of this opposition, the prophet had a word from YHWH that is recorded in Isaiah 66:6–16. This prophetic oracle is theologically sound when set within a context in which those who are faithful to YHWH suffer oppression at the hands of those who are opposed to the rule of YHWH. YHWH speaks "from the temple," and his shout announces the beginning of retribution against the enemies of faith. Not only is there the element of punishment of wrongdoers (14b–16), but there are also words of encouragement, vindication, and hope for faithful believers (7–14a).

> "In this verse (v. 5), the seriously devout are warned that they may expect rejection at the hands of their opponents, who prattle about Yahweh but whose phoniness is evident. Thus the text affirms that right practice of faith is a costly affair. Its proponents can expect to be treated negatively."—Walter Brueggemann, *Isaiah 40–66*, Westminster Bible Companion, 253.

God's Steadfast Love

One aspect of the defeat of evil will be the demonstration of God's steadfast love toward the faithful. This demonstration will be part of the "newness" that YHWH had promised the covenant community (Isa. 65:17). In responding to the needs of the embattled community, YHWH will do things that had never been heard of or seen before (66:8). New life will be given to the community swiftly and dramatically. Before labor pains can begin, the birth process will be complete. YHWH appears as a divine midwife delivering individuals into the community before Mother Zion can feel any pain. There will be only joy! Like Pharaoh of old had been fooled by the midwives Shiphrah and Puah (Ex. 1:15–20), so the enemies of YHWH will fail to destroy the covenant community because of the amazing speed of the births that occur in YHWH's delivery room.

The transformation of life within the community of faith is not limited to the moment of birth. YHWH not only promises amazing additions for the numerical growth of the faithful community, but also assures the believers that the religious community (Jerusalem) will provide abundant love and nurture for the spiritual growth and strengthening of the people of God (vv. 10–11). The prophet's words urge a faithful group that mourns the current suffering of the community not to give up hope. A new day is coming. Third Isaiah, like Jesus, declares, "Blessed are those who mourn, for they will be comforted" (Matt. 5:4).

This new day for the "city of God" will witness the fulfillment of all those prophetic promises that Jerusalem would receive security, wealth, and honor as all nations flood her with tribute (v. 12). The fulfillment of these promises, however, does not depend on any frantic activity of the people. They are but infants who are nursed, carried, and entertained. The new age will not be ushered in by the building of the temple or any other human achievement. It is entirely the work of YHWH. Third Isaiah emphasizes this point in verse 13. No longer is Zion/Jerusalem the mother of the community of faithful, individual believers. YHWH is the mother! The imagery is not consistent. The verse requires mental gymnastics on the part of the reader. There is no smooth transition; there is no easy explanation. Nevertheless, we know that the verse is true and necessary. The faithful believers are not merely children of Jerusalem. We are not simply products of the church. We are the children of God. By God's grace, we are born into the family of God. Third Isaiah expresses this truth through the daring imagery of YHWH as mother: God is the source of life for the community of believers!

The Punishment of Evildoers

The second aspect of YHWH's retribution, according to Third Isaiah, will be the punishment of evildoers, those who are guilty of oppressing God's people (vv. 14b–16). The metaphor for YHWH changes from mother to warrior. The divine warrior is capable of indignation, anger, and fury. YHWH's fierce execution of judgment is expressed in terms of fire, whirlwind, flames of fire, and sword. The victory of God necessarily means the defeat of evil. The destruction of evil will be devastatingly swift and violent as an ambush, a tornado, or an inferno. The scale of judgment is complete: it will be "on all flesh" (v. 16). This picture of judgment affirms YHWH's universal control of history. Once again, within the context of the oppression of YHWH's faithful at the hands of those who are opposed to the rule of YHWH, this word of retribution and judgment is theologically sound and needs to be heard.

If the opponents, however, are composed of fellow believers who hold a different view on some issue (such as the building of a temple), are such violent words of destruction justified? It may be "natural to take comfort in the vision of God paying back his anger in fury" (Hanson, 252), and we may agree that "all such moral indignation in the name of Yahweh is characteristically shot through with self-interest" (Brueggemann, *Isaiah 40–66*, 257), but in this case is it justified? If the opponents are guilty of a syncretism between Israel's faith and a mystery religion that would ultimately destroy Judaism itself (see v. 17), perhaps such drastic language would be necessary. It is possible, however, that the division before Third Isaiah is related to the different theological positions that led to later schisms in Judaism which included the Pharisees and the Essenes. In that case, Brueggemann is right to read the whole passage as "a warning about the church taking itself too seriously on any issue. The awesomeness of Yahweh, who fills heaven and occupies earth, assures that every church agenda—liturgical, doctrinal, moral—is deeply penultimate and does not deserve the passion of ultimacy" (Brueggemann, 252). Extreme caution must be observed when we are tempted to identify our opponents with the enemies of God!

Nevertheless, this chapter brings into focus an even larger source of theological conflict, the question about inclusion within the people of God. If the temple is not able to contain YHWH, and if the vastness of the heavens forms only the throne of YHWH, and if the whole earth is only the footstool of YHWH, and if the judgment of YHWH will be executed upon all flesh, then are the people of YHWH to be limited to the political borders of a Persian province called Judah? If the joyful, miraculous activity of YHWH will result in a new kind of birth, who will be the children of YHWH? If YHWH's plans include a new

> "I am coming to gather all nations and tongues; and they shall come and see my glory. . ."—Isaiah 66:18.

101

heaven and a new earth (v. 22), who will inhabit the new creation? Third Isaiah's answer is radical: "All flesh shall come to worship before me, says the LORD" (v. 23).

All the People of God

The prophet's answer is radical in comparison to the policies of Ezra and Nehemiah, which come from this general period. It is not, however, without precedence in both the Isaiah tradition and the Hebrew Bible as a whole. YHWH's inclusive concern for people beyond Israel already had been forcefully stated in the Isaiah tradition. Isaiah 19:24–25 shows the universal scope of YHWH's election: "On that day Israel will be the third with Egypt and Assyria, a blessing in the midst of the earth, whom the LORD of hosts has blessed, saying, 'Blessed be Egypt my people, and Assyria the work of my hands, and Israel my heritage.'" The universal love of YHWH for all people finds expression at the very beginning of the traditions of Israel. Genesis 12:2–3 portrays it as the very purpose behind the call of Abram: "I will make of you a great nation, and I will bless you, and make your name great, so that you will be a blessing. I will bless those who bless you, and the one who curses you I will curse; and in you all the families of the earth shall be blessed." The author of the book of Jonah, roughly contemporary with Third Isaiah, was also eager to make the point that YHWH's saving activity is directed toward all nations, and Israel, in spite of itself, is to be the messenger of that good news.

"There is no longer Jew or Greek, there is no longer slave or free, there is no longer male and female; for all of you are one in Christ Jesus."—Galatians 3:28.

The uniqueness of this passage is Third Isaiah's expression of the equality among all those who make up the people of God. Verse 18 sounds as if it could be the prelude to another pronouncement of judgment upon the nations. YHWH knows the works and even the thoughts of all people. YHWH is about to gather all nations and tongues. YHWH's glory is about to be displayed. YHWH's glory, however, will not be displayed by inflicting punishment upon the nations or parading them as prisoners of war. Rather, it will be through making them aware of YHWH's glorious presence throughout creation.

Missionaries will be sent to the ends of the earth. Tarshish was a port city in Spain known to Phoenician traders. Put (Pul in the

Hebrew text) and Lud were known from Africa. Tubal (Tabal in Assyrian inscriptions) was located near the southern shores of the Black Sea. It is possible that the phrase "which draw the bow" (*moshkê qeshet*), may have arisen from a misunderstanding of the place-name of Meshech (Muski in Assyrian inscriptions), which is also south of the Black Sea. Tubal and Meshech appear together in Ezekiel 38:2 and 39:1. Javan was a name for Greece. The message of YHWH's glory will be spread to these distant lands and to other, farther shores (v. 19)!

The work of these missionaries will not be unfruitful. Believers will come from these places to Jerusalem as new brothers and sisters in the community of faith (v. 20). Then in two surprising statements of equality, Third Isaiah declares that these believers, just like the Israelites, will bring acceptable offerings to the temple (v. 20), and out of this group YHWH will call some as priests and as Levites (v. 21)! Third Isaiah's vision foreshadows that which was expressed by the former Pharisee Paul, "There is no longer Jew or Greek, there is no longer slave or free, there is no longer male and female; for all of you are one in Christ Jesus" (Gal. 3:28). It is the vision of a covenant people not marked by nationality, but by faith. It is the radically inclusive vision of a time when "all flesh shall come to worship before me, says the LORD" (v. 23).

> "Then, as the ultimate imagery of inclusiveness, in verse 21 it is asserted that from among these *goyim*, these Gentile nations, some will be designated and ordained as priests and Levites. . . . The vision is as large and comprehensive as the invitation to Pentecost (Acts 12:1–13)."—Walter Brueggemann, *Isaiah 40–66*, Westminster Bible Companion, 259.

A Final Warning

Now if the book of Isaiah ended with 66:23, we would be impressed by such a positive, uplifting vision. In reality, we are faced at the end of the book of Isaiah with dead bodies, worms, and unquenchable fire (v. 24). Why? Is this the Bible's first view of hell? Is it, as Brueggemann suggests, evidence of a bitterness between religious rivals whose hatred for each other has grown to such proportions that the simple death of one's enemies will not suffice? "They must keep dying, end-

> "The shocking imagery of the concluding verse states emphatically the dire seriousness of human beings cutting themselves off from the living God. It thus casts in bold relief the miracle that remains the centerpiece of the Book of Isaiah: Those who trust in God will be delivered from bondage and will be established in righteousness."—Paul D. Hanson, *Isaiah 40–66*, Interpretation, 252.

lessly destroyed, perpetually humiliated, everlastingly remembered scornfully" (Brueggemann, *Isaiah 40–66,* 260). Do we have here an unfinished argument between two Jewish parties about inclusion into the people of God? A kind of a "Yes, but . . ." ending that demonstrates that religious bickering has no ending because the other guy always tries to get in the last word? Or is it, as Hanson suggests, the vision's way of expressing "emphatically the dire seriousness of human beings cutting themselves off from the living God" (Hanson, *Isaiah 40–66,* 252)? The seriousness of rebellion against YHWH was in the very first verse of the proclamation of Isaiah of Jerusalem (1:2), and it is fitting that a warning from YHWH against joining those "who have rebelled against me" (66:24) would be the very last verse of the proclamation within the Isaiah tradition.

Nevertheless, the modern reader may well be grateful for an ancient scribe whose sentiments were similar to our own. This scribe made a suggestion in a Masoretic notation that has become part of Jewish tradition whenever this passage is read within the synagogue. After Isaiah 66:24 has been read, Isaiah 66:23 should be read once again. Perhaps this tradition is not simply a desire to end with a promise rather than a curse. Perhaps it is to engage the reader and hearer in the choice that confronts us all with the first reading of verses 23 and 24. To repeat verse 23 is to make our choice known. It functions as a covenant renewal. "As for me and my household, we will serve the LORD" (Josh. 24:15).

Want to Know More?

About the importance of temples to ancient Jews? See R. E. Clements, *Jeremiah,* Interpretation (Atlanta: John Knox Press, 1988), 43–45; Horst Dietrich Preuss, *Old Testament Theology,* vol. 2, 39–51.

? Questions for Reflection

1. Compare Isaiah 66 to Isaiah 44:9–20, the focus of unit 8. How is the debate over building a temple to the Lord similar to the condemnation of idols? How is it different?

2. Has your church or denomination struggled with an issue similar to the one Third Isaiah faced—a "triumphal theology of success and prosperity based on something external and material rather than faith in YHWH alone"?

3. What is true worship? Form small groups of two to three people and describe your ideal worship: the setting, the music (or lack thereof), the elements of worship, the makeup of your fellow worshipers, and so forth.
4. What do you think are the main themes of the book of Isaiah after these ten units of study? How have these scripture passages informed your view of God's people? Of God? Of yourself? Of the contemporary church?

Bibliography

Bright, John. *The Authority of the Old Testament*. Grand Rapids: Baker Book House, 1967.

Brueggemann, Walter. *Isaiah 1–39*. Louisville, Ky.: Westminster John Knox Press, 1998.

_____. *Isaiah 40–66*. Louisville, Ky.: Westminster John Knox Press, 1998.

_____. *Theology of the Old Testament: Testimony, Dispute, Advocacy*. Minneapolis: Fortress Press, 1997.

Childs, Brevard S. *Isaiah*. Old Testament Library. Louisville, Ky.: Westminster John Knox Press, 2000.

Clines, David A. J., ed. *The Dictionary of Classical Hebrew*, vol. 2. Sheffield: Sheffield Academic Press, 1995.

Dillard, Annie. *Teaching a Stone to Talk: Expeditions and Encounters*. New York: Harper & Row, 1982.

Eichrodt, Walther. *Theology of the Old Testament*, vol. 1, Translated by J. A. Baker. Philadelphia: Westminster Press, 1961.

Gerstenberger, Erhard S. *Psalms, Part 1, with an Introduction to Cultic Poetry*. Grand Rapids: Wm. B. Eerdmans Publishing Co., 1988.

Hanson, Paul D. *Isaiah 40–66*. (Louisville, Ky.: John Knox Press, 1995.

Holladay, William L. *Isaiah: Scroll of a Prophetic Heritage*. Grand Rapids: Wm. B. Eerdmans Publishing Co., 1978.

Janzen, J. Gerald. *Job*. Atlanta: John Knox Press, 1985.

Kaiser, Otto. *Isaiah 13–39*. Philadelphia: Westminster Press, 1974.

Knight, George A. F. *Deutero-Isaiah: A Theological Commentary on Isaiah 40–55*. New York: Abingdon Press, 1965.

Lewis, C. S. *The Lion, the Witch, and the Wardrobe*. New York: Collier Books, 1970.

Long, Thomas G. *Matthew*. Westminster Bible Companion. Louisville, Ky.: Westminster John Knox Press, 1997.

Mays, James L. *Psalms*. Interpretation. Louisville, Ky.: John Knox Press, 1994.

Miller, J. Maxwell, and John H. Hayes. *A History of Ancient Israel and Judah*. Philadelphia: Westminster Press, 1986. The quotation of Sennacherib on p. 361 is from James Pritchard, *Ancient Near Eastern Texts Relating to the*

Old Testament, 3d ed., pp. 287–88. Princeton, N.J.: Princeton University Press, 1969.

Oswalt, John N. *Isaiah 1–39.* New International Commentary on the Old Testament. Grand Rapids: Wm. B. Eerdmans Publishing Co., 1986.

Preuss, Horst Dietrich. *Old Testament Theology,* vol. 2. Translated by Leo G. Perdue. Louisville, Ky.: Westminster John Knox Press, 1996.

Seitz, Christopher R. *Isaiah 1–39.* Interpretation. Louisville, Ky.: John Knox Press, 1993.

Smart, James D. *History and Theology in Second Isaiah.* Philadelphia: Westminster Press, 1965.

Sweeney, Marvin A. *Isaiah 1–39: With an Introduction to Prophetic Literature.* The Forms of the Old Testament Literature. Grand Rapids: Wm. B. Eerdmans Publishing Co., 1996.

Westermann, Claus. *Isaiah 40–66,* Translated by David M. G. Stalker. Old Testament Library. Philadelphia: Westminster Press, 1977.

Wildberger, Hans. *Isaiah 1–12,* Translated by Thomas H. Trapp. Continental Commentaries. Minneapolis: Fortress Press, 1991.

Zimmerli, Walther. *Old Testament Theology in Outline.* Translated by David E. Green. Atlanta: John Knox Press, 1978.

Interpretation Bible Studies
Leader's Guide

Interpretation Bible Studies (IBS), for adults and older youth, are flexible, attractive, easy-to-use, and filled with solid information about the Bible. IBS helps Christians discover the guidance and power of the scriptures for living today. Perhaps you are leading a church school class, a mid-week Bible study group, or a youth group meeting, or simply using this in your own personal study. Whatever the setting may be, we hope you find this *Leader's Guide* helpful. Since every context and group is different, this *Leader's Guide* does not presume to tell you how to structure Bible study for your situation. Instead, the *Leader's Guide* seeks to offer choices—a number of helpful suggestions for leading a successful Bible study using IBS.

> "The church that no longer hears the essential message of the Scriptures soon ceases to understand what it is for and is open to be captured by the dominant religious philosophy of the moment."—James D. Smart, *The Strange Silence of the Bible in the Church: A Study in Hermeneutics* (Philadelphia: Westminster Press, 1970), 10.

How Should I Teach IBS?

1. Explore the Format

There is a wealth of information in IBS, perhaps more than you can use in one session. In this case, more is better. IBS has been designed to give you a well-stocked buffet of content and teachable insights. Pick and choose what suits your group's needs. Perhaps you will want to split units into two or more sessions, or combine units into a single session. Perhaps you will decide to use only a portion of a unit and then move on to the next unit. *There is not a structured theme or teaching focus to each unit that must be followed for IBS to be used.* Rather, IBS offers the flexibility to adjust to whatever suits your context.

A recent survey of both professional and volunteer church educators revealed that their number one concern was that Bible study materials be teacher-friendly. IBS is, indeed teacher-friendly in two important ways. First, since IBS provides abundant content and a flexible design, teachers can shape the lessons creatively, responding to the needs of the group and employing a wide variety of teaching methods. Second, those who wish more specific suggestions for planning the sessions can find them at the Geneva Press web site on the Internet (**www.ppcpub.org**). Click the "Free Downloads" button to access teaching suggestions for each IBS unit as well as helpful quotations, selections from Bible dictionaries and encyclopedias, and other teaching helps.

IBS is not only teacher-friendly, it is also discussion-friendly. Given the opportunity, most adults and young people relish the chance to talk about the kind of issues raised in IBS. The secret, then, is to determine what works with your group, what will get them to talk. Several good methods for stimulating discussion are presented in this *Leader's Guide,* and once you learn your group, you can apply one of these methods and get the group discussing the Bible and its relevance in their lives.

The format of every IBS unit consists of several features:

a. Body of the Unit. This is the main content, consisting of interesting and informative commentary on the passage and scholarly insight into the biblical text and its significance for Christians today.

b. Sidebars. These are boxes that appear scattered throughout the body of the unit, with maps, photos, quotations, and intriguing ideas. Some sidebars can be identified quickly by a symbol, or icon, that helps the reader know what type of information can be found in that sidebar. There are icons for illustrations, key terms, pertinent quotes, and more.

c. Want to Know More? Each unit includes a "Want to Know More?" section that guides learners who wish to dig deeper and consult other resources. If your church library does not have the resources mentioned, you can look up the information in other standard Bible dictionaries, encyclopedias, and handbooks, or you can find much of this information at the Geneva Press Web site (see last page of this Guide).

d. Questions for Reflection. The unit ends with questions to help the learners think more deeply about the biblical passage and its pertinence for today. These questions are provided as examples only, and teachers are encouraged both to develop their own list of questions and to gather questions from the group. These discussion questions do not usually have specific "correct" answers. Again, the flexibility of IBS allows you to use these questions at the end of the group time, at the beginning, interspersed throughout, or not at all.

> "The trick is to make the Bible our book."— Duncan S. Ferguson, *Bible Basics: Mastering the Content of the Bible* (Louisville, Ky.: Westminster John Knox Press, 1995), 3.

2. Select a Teaching Method

Here are ten suggestions. The format of IBS allows you to choose what direction you will take as you plan to teach. Only you will know how your lesson should best be designed for your group. Some adult groups prefer the lecture method, while others prefer a high level of free-ranging discussion. Many youth groups like interaction, activity, the use of music, and the chance to talk about their own experiences and feelings. Here is a list of a few possible approaches. Let your own creativity add to the list!

a. Let's Talk about What We've Learned. In this approach, all group members are requested to read the scripture passage and the IBS unit before the group meets. Ask the group members to make notes about the main issues, concerns, and questions they see in the passage. When the group meets, these notes are collected, shared, and discussed. This method depends, of course, on the group's willingness to do some "homework."

b. What Do We Want and Need to Know? This approach begins by having the whole group read the scripture passage together. Then, drawing from your study of the IBS, you, as the teacher, write on a board or flip chart two lists:

(1) Things we should know to better understand this passage (content information related to the passage, for example, historical insights about political contexts, geographical landmarks, economic nuances, etc.), and

> "Although small groups can meet for many purposes and draw upon many different resources, the one resource which has shaped the life of the Church more than any other throughout its long history has been the Bible." —Roberta Hestenes, *Using the Bible in Groups* (Philadelphia: Westminster Press, 1983), 14.

(2) Four or five "important issues we should talk about regarding this passage" (with implications for today— how the issues in the biblical context continue into today, for example, issues of idolatry or fear).

Allow the group to add to either list, if they wish, and use the lists to lead into a time of learning, reflection, and discussion. This approach is suitable for those settings where there is little or no advanced preparation by the students.

c. Hunting and Gathering. Start the unit by having the group read the scripture passage together. Then divide the group into smaller clusters (perhaps having as few as one person), each with a different assignment. Some clusters can discuss one or more of the "Questions for Reflection." Others can look up key terms or people in a Bible dictionary or track down other biblical references found in the body of the unit. After the small clusters have had time to complete their tasks, gather the entire group again and lead them through the study material, allowing each cluster to contribute what it learned.

d. From Question Mark to Exclamation Point. This approach begins with contemporary questions and then moves to the biblical content as a response to those questions. One way to do this is for you to ask the group, at the beginning of the class, a rephrased version of one or more of the "Questions for Reflection" at the end of the study unit. For example, one of the questions at the end of the unit on Exodus 3:1–4:17 in the IBS *Exodus* volume reads,

> Moses raised four protests, or objections, to God's call. Contemporary people also raise objections to God's call. In what ways are these similar to Moses' protests? In what ways are they different?

This question assumes familiarity with the biblical passage about Moses, so the question would not work well before the group has explored the passage. However, try rephrasing this question as an opening exercise; for example:

Here is a thought experiment: Let's assume that God, who called people in the Bible to do daring and risky things, still calls people today to tasks of faith and courage. In the Bible, God called Moses from a burning bush and called Isaiah in a moment of ecstatic worship in the Temple. How do you think God's call is experienced by people today? Where do you see evidence of people saying "yes" to God's call? When people say "no" or raise an objection to God's call, what reasons do they give (to themselves, to God)?

Posing this or a similar question at the beginning will generate discussion and raise important issues, and then it can lead the group into an exploration of the biblical passage as a resource for thinking even more deeply about these questions.

e. Let's Go to the Library. From your church library, your pastor's library, or other sources, gather several good commentaries on the book of the Bible you are studying. Among the trustworthy commentaries are those in the Interpretation series (John Knox Press) and the Westminster Bible Companion series (Westminster John Knox Press). Divide your group into smaller clusters and give one commentary to each cluster (one or more of the clusters can be given the IBS volume instead of a full-length commentary). Ask each cluster to read the biblical passage you are studying and then to read the section of the commentary that covers that passage (if your group is large, you may want to make photocopies of the commentary material with proper permission, of course). The task of each cluster is to name the two or three most important insights they discover about the biblical passage by reading and talking together about the commentary material. When you reassemble the larger group to share these insights, your group will gain not only a variety of insights about the passage but also a sense that differing views of the same text are par for the course in biblical interpretation.

f. Working Creatively Together. Begin with a creative group task, tied to the main thrust of the study. For example, if the study is on the Ten Commandments, a parable, or a psalm, have the group rewrite the Ten Commandments, the parable, or the psalm in contemporary language. If the passage is an epistle, have the group write a letter to their own congregation. Or if the study is a narrative, have the group role-play the characters in the story or write a page describing the story from the point of view of one of the characters. After completion of the task, read and discuss the biblical passage,

113

asking for interpretations and applications from the group and tying in IBS material as it fits the flow of the discussion.

g. Singing Our Faith. Begin the session by singing (or reading) together a hymn that alludes to the biblical passage being studied (or to the theological themes in the passage). Most hymnals have an index of scriptural allusions. For example, if you are studying the unit from the IBS volume on Psalm 121, you can sing "I to the Hills Will Lift My Eyes," "Sing Praise to God, Who Reigns Above," or another hymn based on Psalm 121. Let the group reflect on the thoughts and feelings evoked by the hymn, then move to the biblical passage, allowing the biblical text and the IBS material to underscore, clarify, refine, and deepen the discussion stimulated by the hymn. If you are ambitious, you may ask the group to write a new hymn at the end of the study! (Many hymnals have indexes in the back or companion volumes that help the user match hymns to scripture passages or topics.)

h. Fill in the Blanks. In order to help the learners focus on the content of the biblical passage, at the beginning of the session ask each member of the group to read the biblical passage and fill out a brief questionnaire about the details of the passage (provide a copy for each learner or write the questions on the board). For example, if you are studying the unit in the IBS *Matthew* volume on Matthew 22:1–14, the questionnaire could include questions such as the following:

—In this story, Jesus compares the kingdom of heaven to what?
—List the various responses of those who were invited to the king's banquet but who did not come.
—When his invitation was rejected, how did the king feel? What did the king do?
—In the second part of the story, when the king saw a man at the banquet without a wedding garment, what did the king say? What did the man say? What did the king do?
—What is the saying found at the end of this story?

Gather the group's responses to the questions and perhaps encourage discussion. Then lead the group through the IBS material helping the learners to understand the meanings of these details and the significance of the passage for today. Feeling creative? Instead of a fill-in-the blanks questionnaire, create a crossword puzzle from names and words in the biblical passage.

i. Get the Picture. In this approach, stimulate group discussion by incorporating a painting, photograph, or other visual object into the lesson. You can begin by having the group examine and comment on this visual or you can introduce the visual later in the lesson—it depends on the object used. If, for example, you are studying the unit Exodus 3:1–4:17 in the IBS *Exodus* volume, you may want to view Paul Koli's very colorful painting *The Burning Bush.* Two sources for this painting are *The Bible Through Asian Eyes,* edited by Masao Takenaka and Ron O'Grady (National City, Calif.: Pace Publishing Co., 1991), and *Imaging the Word: An Arts and Lectionary Resource,* vol. 3, edited by Susan A. Blain (Cleveland: United Church Press, 1996).

j. Now Hear This. Especially if your class is large, you may want to use the lecture method. As the teacher, you prepare a presentation on the biblical passage, using as many resources as you have available plus your own experience, but following the content of the IBS unit as a guide. You can make the lecture even more lively by asking the learners at various points along the way to refer to the visuals and quotes found in the "sidebars." A place can be made for questions (like the ones at the end of the unit)—either at the close of the lecture or at strategic points along the way.

> "It is . . . important to call a Bible study group back to what the text being discussed actually says, especially when an individual has gotten off on some tangent." —Richard Robert Osmer, *Teaching for Faith: A Guide for Teachers of Adult Classes* (Louisville, Ky.: Westminster John Knox Press, 1992), 71.

3. Keep These Teaching Tips in Mind

There are no surefire guarantees for a teaching success. However, the following suggestions can increase the chances for a successful study:

a. Always Know Where the Group Is Headed. Take ample time beforehand to prepare the material. Know the main points of the study, and know the destination. Be flexible, and encourage discussion, but don't lose sight of where you are headed.

b. Ask Good Questions; Don't Be Afraid of Silence. Ideally, a discussion blossoms spontaneously from the reading of the scripture. But more often than not, a discussion must be drawn from the group members by a series of well-chosen questions. After asking each

115

question, give the group members time to answer. Let them think, and don't be threatened by a season of silence. Don't feel that every question must have an answer, and that as leader, you must supply every answer. Facilitate discussion by getting the group members to cooperate with each other. Sometimes, the original question can be restated. Sometimes it is helpful to ask a follow-up question like "What makes this a hard question to answer?"

Ask questions that encourage explanatory answers. Try to avoid questions that can be answered simply "Yes" or "No." Rather than asking, "Do you think Moses was frightened by the burning bush?" ask, "What do you think Moses was feeling and experiencing as he stood before the burning bush?" If group members answer with just one word, ask a follow-up question like "Why do you think this is so?" Ask questions about their feelings and opinions, mixed within questions about facts or details. Repeat their responses or restate their response to reinforce their contributions to the group.

> "Studies of learning reveal that while people remember approximately 10% of what they hear, they remember up to 90% of what they say. Therefore, to increase the amount of learning that occurs, increase the amount of talking about the Bible which each member does."—Roberta Hestenes, *Using the Bible in Groups* (Philadelphia: Westminster Press, 1983), 17.

Most studies can generate discussion by asking open-ended questions. Depending on the group, several types of questions can work. Some groups will respond well to content questions that can be answered from reading the IBS comments or the biblical passage. Others will respond well to questions about feelings or thoughts. Still others will respond to questions that challenge them to new thoughts or that may not have exact answers. Be sensitive to the group's dynamic in choosing questions.

Some suggested questions are: What is the point of the passage? Who are the main characters? Where is the tension in the story? Why does it say (this)_____, and not (that) _____? What raises questions for you? What terms need defining? What are the new ideas? What doesn't make sense? What bothers or troubles you about this passage? What keeps you from living the truth of this passage?

c. Don't Settle for the Ordinary. There is nothing like a surprise. Think of special or unique ways to present the ideas of the study. Upset the applecart of the ordinary. Even though the passage may be familiar, look for ways to introduce suspense. Remember that a little mystery can capture the imagination. Change your routine.

Along with the element of surprise, humor can open up a discussion. Don't be afraid to laugh. A well-chosen joke or cartoon may present the central theme in a way that a lecture would have stymied.

Sometimes a passage is too familiar. No one speaks up because everyone feels that all that could be said has been said. Choose an unfamiliar translation from which to read, or if the passage is from a Gospel, compare the story across two or more Gospels and note differences. It is amazing what insights can be drawn from seeing something strange in what was thought to be familiar.

d. Feel Free to Supplement the IBS Resources with Other Material. Consult other commentaries or resources. Tie in current events with the lesson. Scour newspapers or magazines for stories that touch on the issues of the study. Sometimes the lyrics of a song, or a section of prose from a well-written novel will be just the right seasoning for the study.

e. And Don't Forget to Check the Web. Check out our site on the World Wide Web (www.ppcpub.org). Click the "Free Downloads" button to access teaching suggestions. Several possibilities for applying the teaching methods suggested above for individual IBS units will be available. Feel free to download this material.

> "The Bible is literature, but it is much more than literature. It is the holy book of Jews and Christians, who find there a manifestation of God's presence." —Kathleen Norris, *The Psalms* (New York: Riverhead Books, 1997), xxii.

f. Stay Close to the Biblical Text. Don't forget that the goal is to learn the Bible. Return to the text again and again. Avoid making the mistake of reading the passage only at the beginning of the study, and then wandering away to comments on top of comments from that point on. Trust in the power and presence of the Holy Spirit to use the truths of the passage to work within the lives of the study participants.

What If I Am Using IBS in Personal Bible Study?

If you are using IBS in your personal Bible study, you can experiment and explore a variety of ways. You may choose to read straight through the study without giving any attention to the sidebars or other features. Or you may find yourself interested in a question or unfamiliar with a key term, and you can allow the sidebars "Want to Know More?" and "Questions for Reflection" to lead you into deeper learning on these issues. Perhaps you will want to have a few commentaries or a Bible dictionary available to pursue what interests you. As was suggested in one of the teaching methods above, you may want to begin with the questions at the end, and then read the Bible passage followed by the IBS material. Trust the IBS resources to provide good and helpful information, and then follow your interests!

Want to Know More?

About leading Bible study groups? See Roberta Hestenes, *Using the Bible in Groups* (Philadelphia: Westminster Press, 1983).

About basic Bible content? See Duncan S. Ferguson, *Bible Basics: Mastering the Content of the Bible* (Louisville, Ky.: Westminster John Knox Press, 1995); William M. Ramsay, *The Westminster Guide to the Books of the Bible* (Louisville, Ky.: Westminster John Knox Press, 1994).

About the development of the Bible? See John Barton, *How the Bible Came to Be* (Louisville, Ky.: Westminster John Knox Press, 1997).

About the meaning of difficult terms? See Donald K. McKim, *Westminster Dictionary of Theological Terms* (Louisville, Ky.: Westminster John Knox Press, 1996); Paul J. Achtemeier, *Harper's Bible Dictionary* (San Francisco: Harper & Row, 1985).

For more information about IBS,

click the "Free Downloads" button at

www.ppcpub.org